When BAD Grammar Happens to GOOD People

HOW TO AVOID COMMON ERRORS IN ENGLISH

ANN BATKO

Edited by Edward Rosenheim

CAREER
PRESS
Franklin Lakes, NJ

WHEN BAD GRAMMAR HAPPENS TO GOOD PEOPLE
EDITED AND TYPESET BY KRISTEN PARKES
Cover design by The Visual Group
Printed in the U.S.A. by Book-mart Press

To order this title, please call toll-free 1-800-CAREER-1 (NJ and Canada: 201-848-0310) to order using VISA or MasterCard, or for further information on books from Career Press.

The Career Press, Inc., 3 Tice Road, PO Box 687,
Franklin Lakes, NJ 07417
www.careerpress.com

Library of Congress Cataloging-in-Publication Data

Batko, Ann.
    When bad grammar happens to good people : how to avoid common errors in English / by Ann Batko ; edited by Edward Rosenheim.
        p. cm.
    Includes index.
    ISBN 1-56414-722-3
        1. English language—Grammar—Handbooks, manuals, etc. 2. English language—Usage—Handbooks, manuals, etc. I. Title.

PE1111.B385 2004
428.2—dc22

                                                            2003069601

To my father,

who never lets go of a good idea.

Acknowledgments

This book has had a long gestation. The idea was inspired by the chapter title "Do You Make These 100 Common Errors in English?" taken from one of the many books written by the late Herbert V. Prochnow, former president of the First National Bank of Chicago.

I am indebted to Edward Rosenheim, the distinguished editor of this book, for the vision and direction he gave at critical points in the planning and writing. I am grateful to Tracy Weiner, associate director of the University of Chicago Writing Program, for creating the various test sections, which provide invaluable reinforcement and a welcome sense of humor. Barbara Stufflebeem, a freelance editor and former student of Edward Rosenheim's, also made valuable contributions to the manuscript.

Author's Note

Everyone has bad language habits. We hear language errors on TV, at work, and even from our family—so many times that the errors might seem correct. But they're still errors, and they can make us sound less sophisticated, or even less intelligent, than we really are.

Fortunately, you can form new, good habits the same way you got stuck with the bad ones: by repetition. This program will help you do it. Here's how:

1. Get started: Find out what you know. A pretest that covers some of the most common language errors is included in this book. If you get an answer wrong, or if you're just not sure why you got it right, the pretest's key will direct you to the chapter—or group of related errors—that can help.

2. Choose where to begin! The chapters are carefully organized in a series. The program works best if you take the units in the order you find them. However, they can stand alone if need be. After you take the pretest, you may want to jump to a particular chapter on a topic of special interest to you.

3. Practice out loud when working through a unit. This will help train your ear to hear what is correct and to get you comfortable using language or phrases that may feel unfamiliar or downright wrong at first.

4. Test yourself to see how far you've come. Each chapter is divided into manageable sections, and each section ends with a test. Take a test when you think you've got a handle on a section's errors. The test's key will let you know whether you've mastered the section.

5. Reinforce what you know. To make your new knowledge a new habit, look for examples of the things you've learned when you're reading the paper, watching TV, or listening to a conversation at work.

6. Test yourself again to make sure a good habit stays stuck. At the end of the book you'll find review tests for the more complex grammatical chapters. To find out if your good habits have really sunk in, you might want to take a chapter's review tests a week or so after you feel you've mastered the material. If you get it right, congratulations! You've formed a good habit!

Contents

Foreword

Language is the great gift that distinguishes human beings from other creatures. Like most gifts, it can be used thoughtfully and to good advantage—or it can be used carelessly, indifferently, and quite unsuccessfully. The way in which you use language can tell people a good deal about your personal qualities—your way of thinking, your alertness, your concern for useful communication with other people—and your concern, your respect, for the English language itself.

When your speech is sloppy, when it seems to reveal that you have never learned—or perhaps just don't care—about using language properly, you certainly don't do yourself any favors. Other people are likely to assume, whether fairly or not, that your thinking has flaws because your language does, and you may, as a result, fail to make the favorable impression that can so often be important. People may assume that, whatever your strong points, you will not fit in well in business or professional or social situations where the proper use of language is taken for granted. Even more seriously, they may be unable even to understand important things you're trying to say because your language is inadequately serving its most basic purpose: to convey clearly what's on your mind. In short, when

17

your language doesn't meet expected standards, you are likely to do serious injustice to your talents and your ideas.

On the bright side, a command of proper English provides a kind of invisible passport into the company of people who, because they respect language, almost automatically respect others who use it correctly. This is true in social gatherings, business conversations, everything from random exchanges to public addresses. In all these circumstances, an awareness that you are meeting common standards of correctness can breed a comfortable self-assurance; you can be quietly confident that your use of language is an asset rather than a liability.

Of course, you will probably not be regularly or strongly aware of speaking "correct English" any more than you are always conscious of conforming to other codes that govern our conduct: ordinary politeness, for example, or adherence to the rules of various games. This means that for the most part it will only be the errors, the lapses in the appropriate use of language, which you will notice in others' speech, or they in yours. This may not be a particularly pleasant fact about human nature, but it's a pretty good reason for embarking on the program set forth in this book.

Like our acceptance and observance of most rules in the conduct of our lives, correct use of language becomes a habit, and it is with the cultivation of this habit that the program is concerned. As we work with habits of speech (eliminating old, undesirable ones; developing new, useful ones), we'll have to rely considerably on "rules" and discuss the "right" and "wrong" ways of saying things, so it is only fair to say before we start that the rules are not universal, timeless laws, inscribed somewhere in stone and to be applied mechanically to determine without question what is right and wrong. Language changes constantly and in many ways. Any student of language knows that words enter and depart from our common vocabulary and, while they do remain in use, they often undergo changes of meaning. Ideas of grammatical correctness also change. And a word or construction commonly accepted in one geographic area or by one particular group of people can be quite foreign to those in other locales or communities, even though all of them are speaking English. This variability is true even of the use each one of us makes of language, for our speaking and writing are frequently adjusted to the circumstances that surround them. If you are like most people, your language at a ball game is different from your language in a committee meeting; your official business letters are not written in precisely the same language as your e-mail messages or letters to your family; and there is considerable difference in the way you address your employer and your language with a 4-year-old child (unless you are particularly rash or you have an unusually dull-witted employer).

This variability in language suggests that we shouldn't be too rigid or stubborn about what is right and wrong, for these are matters that many circumstances can change or modify. (Professional students of language can systematically study such changes, so that a thorough knowledge of language includes much insight into the processes of change themselves.) But although language changes, and although there is no absolute, permanent definition of correctness, we can take as our guide language that experienced and careful speakers accept as correct. We can determine what is "right" and "wrong" about our use of language by learning principles that will help us recognize this established standard. To put it bluntly: While some of the rules for correct English may be impermanent and relative, don't try this theory out on potential customers or clients or employers, who may be quite naturally put off by what they regard as your improper (or inappropriate or uneducated) use of English.

The fact is that, at any particular time, it is possible to speak of specific uses of language, not as eternally correct, but as "accepted," as conforming to what the great *New Oxford English Dictionary* simply calls "the standard of literature and conversation." The standards are those applied by the compilers of dictionaries (many of whom today go so far as to classify words under such headings as "formal," "conversational," "slang," and even "vulgar"). The standards are set by various experts on language who in turn rely, at least in part, on the practices of a great many diversified but responsible speakers and writers. These experts can certainly disagree; most of them would be among the first to insist that their findings are subject to change and challenge. But what they do is to record a consensus as to the "right" choice to be made by those of us who, for good reason, seek to use language with precision, clarity, and force.

EDWARD W. ROSENHEIM
Professor Emeritus
University of Chicago,
Department of English Language and Literature

How Do We Learn to Speak Correctly?

You know more about good grammar than you may think. To illustrate, choose the right word in the following statement:

Yesterday I (go, went) to the store.

The correct choice is "went." Almost everybody who grew up speaking English will get that right. But *why* did you get it right? If you are a native English speaker, you didn't need the official grammar rule: To express the indicative past tense in the first person, use the indicative first person past tense of the verb with the first-person pronoun. "Went" just "sounded" correct.

But that didn't happen by magic. You learned this grammatical principle a long time ago, and you learned it the natural way: by repetition. The adults around you spoke like that (if they spoke English). You imitated them, and they corrected you when you got it wrong. You didn't have to lug around a grammar book when you were 3 years old, but you still learned when to say "went." It became a habit.

Unfortunately, not all the language habits we learn are good ones. You probably hear language errors all the time: on TV, in schools, in the workplace, or from family and friends. So like everyone, you've probably formed some bad habits, habits that can be disastrous when it's important to speak correctly. People judge you by the way you speak, and they can dismiss what you have to say if you say it carelessly. They might conclude that you lack the professional polish to do a certain kind of job, or miss your point altogether because of mistakes or verbal clutter in your manner of speaking.

This book will help you unlearn those bad language habits and learn good ones. Grammar and usage principles are explained along the way—you need to know the rules in order to understand why a sentence is right or wrong—but knowing the rules isn't enough. Here's one rule, for example, that many find confusing:

> Use the subjective case of the relative pronoun "who/whom" as the subject of a verb or after a finite form of the verb "to be"; use the objective case of the relative pronoun "who/whom" as the object of a verb, the indirect object of a verb, the subject of an infinitive, the object of an infinitive, or the object of a preposition.

Now that you've seen the rule, try answering the following question:

> Unfortunately, the person (who, whom) Frank believed was his new secretary proved to be the efficiency expert hired to evaluate his grammar.

The correct answer is "who": it's the subject of the verb "was" (not, incidentally, the object of the verb "believed"). If you had trouble figuring it out, don't worry. Knowing the rule is helpful, but you need practice, too, along with some useful tips for making the complicated rules memorable. That is just what this program will give you. The rules of grammar and usage have been incorporated into a user-friendly package that will help you to learn the "official" rules, and reinforce your understanding through short-cut tips in many cases, and then you can test yourself on numerous examples.

What Kind of Errors Does This Program Include?

Many reference books on grammar and usage address thousands of topics, some of them so obscure that they never come up in daily life. But this book is a more focused program that will help you make the most of your time. Rather than cover every possible problem, two criteria were used to decide whether or not to include an error:

1. *Is the error one that will suggest to others that your language isn't quite what it could be?* If you misuse the word "immanent," only a few theologians and philosophers will be able to catch the error or care that you've made it. But if you mix up the verbs "lay" and "lie," many people at work or in social situations will think that you use language carelessly.

2. *Is the error one of the mistakes that people make most often?* This book includes the errors that give the most difficulty to the most people. That doesn't mean that every individual makes all these mistakes. Because each of us learns the language differently at home and at school, you'll probably find some errors that seem laughably obvious to you, along with others that you are surprised to learn are incorrect. And you may not find a few of the errors that concern you. That's because some errors, while important, are pretty rare—accidental products of the way that one particular individual learned the language. One of the editors of this book, for example, mispronounced the word "novel" until she was 22, when some kind person finally pointed it out to her. But because not many people make this error, it hasn't been included, however much psychological damage it caused our editor in her youth. So while not every mistake you've ever made will appear here, you'll be able resolve the most important problems most people have with the language.

The mistakes we include fall into three broad classes: grammar, usage, and pronunciation.

1. **Grammar** refers to the fundamental principles and structure of the language, including clear and correct sentence construction and the proper forms of words. This category includes mixing up transitive and intransitive verbs (such as "lie" vs. "lay"), mixing up the correct forms of pronouns (such as "who" vs. "whom"), and using a verb that doesn't agree with its subject (as in "Everyone are going to the store").

2. **Usage** refers to the way that particular words are used. Such errors include mixing up words that sound alike (such as "affect" vs. "effect"), mixing up words whose meanings are related (such as "imply" vs. "infer"), using made-up words (such as "irregardless"), and using so-called clutter expressions that don't add anything to your meaning (such as "at that point in time").

3. **Pronunciation** problems are important because mispronouncing a word will definitely affect the way people perceive you. In Chapter 13, you'll see the correct pronunciations of some of the most frequently mispronounced words in English, such as "nuclear."

How This Program Is Organized

You can start the program by taking a test! No, don't run away. The **Pretest** that follows this introduction is designed to save you some time; it will help you identify what you need to work on most. The Pretest's key will let you know where in the program to look for help on anything you get wrong or find difficult.

To remind you of some of the basic vocabulary you'll need in order to follow the lessons, a **Grammar Review** has been included at the beginning of the book. But you don't necessarily have to attack this first. You can read right through it if you'd like, or you can go straight to the errors themselves, and refer back to the Grammar Review if the lessons contain a term you don't understand. If you think the "imperative mood" is something your mother was in when she insisted that you do your chores, you'll find the Grammar Review helpful.

To break up the program into manageable chunks, the errors have been grouped into units related to a specific area of difficulty, such as tricky verbs or subject/verb agreement. These units are arranged in a logical order that will allow you to progress from less complicated concepts to more complicated ones. Because each chapter is self-contained, it's possible to jump directly to the errors that most interest you. If the Pretest lets you know that you have trouble with subject/verb agreement, for example, you can jump right to Chapter 3 and learn all about it. But it is strongly suggested that you work only on one chapter at a time, and to consider taking the chapters in order. You'll get better and faster results if you progress through groups of closely related errors.

To make it easier for you to work through each chapter, they've been subdivided into sections containing errors that can be traced back to one grammar or usage rule. The unit on verbs, for example, contains a section on transitive vs. intransitive verbs, a section on tricky verb tenses, and a section on the subjunctive. The sections will begin with a brief lesson explaining the rule, and then will address the individual errors.

The individual errors are easy to find because they are numbered for quick reference. They follow a fairly consistent pattern. You'll find:

- ❑ A brief **lesson** in some sections to give you some basic concepts.

- ❑ The **number** and **name** of the error.

- ❑ A sample of an incorrect sentence headed by **Don't Say**. If this sentence sounds right to you, you'll know it's a bad habit you'll have to unlearn, and that you'll need to pay extra attention to this entry.

- ❑ A corrected sentence headed by **Say Instead**.
- ❑ A **Here's Why** section that explains the basic rule or usage guideline, which may be anywhere from a sentence to a few paragraphs long, depending on how complicated the topic is.
- ❑ **Additional sentence examples** to help you remember the correct form.
- ❑ A **tip**, on occasion, to help you remember the rule.

To help you review and measure your progress, there is a **Test** at the end of each section in all the chapters except the one on pronunciation. You'll find the answers in a key at the end of the test. You should take the tests when you feel you've mastered the contents of a section.

Finally, to help you determine whether you've really formed a new habit, additional **Review Tests** (with answer keys) are included at the end of the manual. These review tests cover the grammatical concepts that people find most difficult. These tests will work best for you if you take them after you've read the chapter more than once and done some practicing out loud. Try waiting a day—or even a week—before taking a chapter's review test. This will let you know whether you've really formed a new habit.

Finally, you may want to retake the Pretest after you've been working with the program for several weeks. This will give you the satisfaction of learning how far you've come!

We hope you'll find this program helpful. "Habit," as the philosopher Michel de Montaigne once said, "is a second nature." If you're committed to forming new habits, we believe that clear and precise language can become second nature to you, allowing you to speak with ease and confidence.

Pretest

Ready for a test? The following sentences cover some of the most common errors in English. If you don't know all the answers, don't worry—the rest of the book can help. At the end of the Pretest you'll find an Answer Key that not only gives the answers, but also refers you to the chapter that will explain each answer for you.

Pretest

Circle the correct choice.

1. Doris foolishly spent four hours (laying, lying) by the pool and now looks like a radish.

2. Each of those revolting insects (belong, belongs) to an endangered species.

3. The insects are no longer (lying, laying) on the table because every one of them (have fallen, has fallen) onto the carpet.

4. Pauline and a man with a large sheepdog (live, lives) in the apartment above mine.

5. My wife and (I, me, myself) have tickets to the submarine races tonight.

6. Harry was begging for disaster when he (set, sat) his new TV on a rickety table, (lay, laid) a glass of milk on the TV, and left the cat alone in the room.

7. I wish I (was, were) skydiving in the Andes alone with you.

8. It's (he, him) who left the laundry out in the rain.

9. We surprised Rudolph and (she, her) with a gala anniversary bash.

10. My grandfather left most of his money to a home for wayward dentists; the rest went directly to my daughter and (I, me, myself).

11. I gave your car keys to the woman (who, whom) you recently sued.

12. I'll give your car keys to (whoever, whomever) asks for them.

13. The machete, (that, which) he'd almost left back at camp, turned out to be critical when Jim was faced with jungle growth (which, that) was too dense to get through on his own.

14. Only Rhonda and the man in the black hat (is, are) doing the tango.

15. Either Phyllis or Leticia (is, are) staying up all night to finish the project.

16. Either Phyllis or the guys in the billing department (is, are) going on an emergency coffee run.

17. I want that pastry so (bad, badly) that I can almost taste it.

18. She spent the next six months looking for someone as (different than, different from) Reginald as possible.

19. Wanda correctly (inferred, implied) from Steve's frantic signals that he meant to (imply, infer) that she should get off the train tracks.

28

20. The motion of the ship had little (affect, effect) on her, but the sudden appearance of her ex-husband on deck (affected, effected) her dramatically.

21. Her story (composes, comprises) many bizarre episodes, each (composed of, comprised of) moments more sordid than the last.

22. To win my love you must meet one simple (criteria, criterion): absolute perfection.

23. We stared (incredibly, incredulously) at the (incredible, incredulous) spectacle of Lulu dancing on the table.

24. I'm going to sell the house and become a cowpoke (irregardless, regardless) of what you say.

25. Angela kept a (respectful, respective) distance from the bears and the wolves, (that, which) eventually retreated to their (respectful, respective) dens.

Answer Key

1. lying. (See Chapter 2—verb tenses.)
2. belongs. (See Chapter 3—agreement.)
3. lying, has fallen. (See Chapter 3—agreement.)
4. live. (See Chapter 3—agreement.)
5. I. (See Chapter 3—agreement.)
6. set, laid. (See Chapter 2—verb tenses.)
7. were. (See Chapter 2—verb tenses.)
8. he. (See Chapter 1—problem pronouns.)
9. her. (See Chapter 1—problem pronouns.)
10. me. (See Chapter 1—problem pronouns.)
11. whom. (See Chapter 1—problem pronouns.)
12. whoever. (See Chapter 1—problem pronouns.)
13. which, that. (See Chapter 1—problem pronouns.)
14. are. (See Chapter 3—agreement.)
15. is. (See Chapter 3—agreement.)

16. are. (See Chapter 3—agreement.)
17. badly. (See Chapter 4—modifiers.)
18. different from. (See Chapter 5—prepositions.)
19. inferred, imply. (See Chapter 8—words that sound the same.)
20. effect, affected. (See Chapter 8—words that sound the same.)
21. comprises, composed of. (See Chapter 8—words that sound the same.)
22. criterion. (See Chapter 7—plurals.)
23. incredulously, incredible. (See Chapter 8—words that sound the same.)
24. regardless. (See Chapter 11—made-up words.)
25. respectful, which, respective. (See Chapter 8—words that sound the same; see also Chapter 1—problem pronouns.)

Grammar Review

Math phobia has a cousin; it's grammar anxiety. The very word, grammar, probably calls up bad memories of being the last person in your 6th grade class to understand what "subordinate clause" means. But the truth is, the basic terminology and concepts of grammar aren't all that hard to master—and understanding them is the surest route to eliminating common grammatical errors from your speech. This review is designed to remind you of those grammar basics if they've slipped away from you since 6th grade or to teach them to you for the first time if you were looking out the window and not paying attention. We're going to cover two basic areas. First, we'll go over the eight parts of speech—nouns, verbs, and so on—and remind you what they are and what roles they play in a sentence. Second, we'll look at the parts of a sentence: subjects, predicates, clauses, and complements, and show you how to tell one from the other.

The Eight Parts of Speech

There are more than 500,000 words in the English language, but fortunately for us students of English grammar, only eight parts of speech. "Part of speech" refers to the part or role that a word plays within a phrase or a sentence—its *function*. We'll look at them in detail in a moment, but here's the 60-second overview of the eight roles words can play:

❏ The function of a **noun** is to name something: a person, a place, an object, or an idea. "Basketball" and "relationship" are nouns.

❏ The function of a **pronoun** is to stand in for a noun. "Which" and "she" are pronouns.

❏ The function of a **verb** is to describe an action or a state of being. "Run" and "is" are verbs.

❏ The function of an **adjective** is to modify the meaning of a noun or pronoun. "Blue" and "cheery" are adjectives.

❏ The function of an **adverb** is to modify the meaning of a verb, an adjective, or another adverb. "Swiftly" and "very" are adverbs.

❏ The function of a **preposition** is to express the relationship between a noun or a pronoun and certain other words in the sentence. "Inside" and "under" are prepositions.

❏ The function of a **conjunction** is to join together words or phrases. "And" and "but" are conjunctions.

❏ The function of an **interjection** is to express excitement and emotion independently from the other words in the sentence. "Hey" and "oh" are interjections.

This idea of *function* is critical when identifying the various parts of speech, because many words have more than one possible role. In other words, you can't simply take our 500,000-plus English words and divide them into eight categories for the various parts of speech. It's a little trickier than that. Some nouns, for example, love to get dressed up and go parading around as verbs and adjectives. Some adverbs and prepositions have passports that allow them to cross each other's borders. And a lot of pronouns moonlight as adjectives. So the important thing is not to think in terms of a permanent relationship between a given word and a part of speech—only some of them believe in "till death do us part"—but instead to look at what role that word is playing in the particular sentence in question.

Here's an example of how one word, in this case, "love," can have several different functions:

As a noun: He wrote a book about <u>love</u>.
As a verb: I <u>love</u> eating out.
As an adjective: She read a <u>love</u> poem.

All right now, roll up your sleeves and let's dig into each of the eight parts of speech. We'll start with nouns, pronouns, and verbs, the parts that really do the heavy lifting within a sentence.

#1: The Noun

A noun is simply a name, a word that identifies whatever it is you're talking about, such as "Jack" or "home" or "rock." You may remember the term "noun" being defined in school as a person, place, or thing. This is a good way to think about it provided you remember that "thing" refers to more than the things you can point to or touch. It also includes intangibles— ideas, concepts, qualities and actions. "Freedom" is a noun. "Progress" is a noun. "Embarrassment" and "running" and "millimeter" are nouns. Basically, anything you can put the word "the" in front of is a noun or is being used as a noun. "Being used as a noun" refers back to the idea that many words can play more than one part of speech. "Light," for example, can be both a noun, as in *the <u>light</u> of day* or a verb, as in *I <u>light</u> the candles*. Just remember that whenever the word in question is being used to name or identify something, you're dealing with a noun.

#2: The Pronoun

Pronouns are words such as "he," "she," "it," and "that," which take the place of nouns so that we don't have to drive each other nuts saying things such as *Harry went to Harry's car and then Harry drove to pick up Susan, and then Harry and Susan drove to Harry's father's house.* Instead, we can use pronouns to refer back to some of the nouns in the sentence, and say, *Harry went to his car and then he drove to pick up Susan, and then they went to his father's house.* If you have trouble remembering the definition, just take the word apart: "pro" means "for" as in "pro-government" or "pro vs. con," so "pronoun" simply means "for a noun."

It would be great if pronouns were no more complicated than that. But they come in all kinds of flavors and varieties designed to handle different assignments within a sentence, and they won't do anything outside of their specific job descriptions. They get all bent out of shape if you make them try. Here's the rundown on the three basic facts you need to understand about pronouns in order to keep them in line.

Pronoun Fact #1: There Are Five Different Kinds

It's not critical to memorize where each and every pronoun falls within these groups, but a quick overview of the following information will give you a framework for understanding what's ahead.

Personal pronouns refer mostly to—you guessed it—persons. They're used to identify the person speaking, the person being spoken to, and the person or thing being spoken about. They're familiar words such as "I," "me," "she," "it," "they," and "you," to name just a handful. Within the larger group of personal pronouns is a subgroup called intensive or reflexive pronouns. These are words such as "myself," "himself," and "themselves." We won't worry any more about the intensive or reflexive variety here, but they do cause trouble sometimes, and you'll find a lesson devoted to them in Chapter 2. Personal pronouns in general are the most complex group and are implicated in more errors than their other pronoun friends. Facts number two and three ahead focus on the two most important complexities of this tribe.

Demonstrative pronouns point out specific persons, places, and things. Luckily, there are only two: "this" and "that." Okay, there are four if you count their plural forms: "these" and "those."

Indefinite pronouns do the opposite job of demonstrative pronouns. They're used when you don't have a particular person, place, or thing to which to refer. This is a big group of pronouns, but a few common ones are "any," "each," "everyone," "nobody," "other," "several," "something," and "nothing."

Relative pronouns relate a person or thing to something that's being said about them. The most common are "who," "whom," "whose," "which," "that," and "what," but there are also compound forms such as "whatever," "whoever," and so on. Relative pronouns are used to introduce a descriptive phrase within a sentence; for example, *Ellen loved the karate class that she took last fall*. The relative pronoun "that" refers back to "karate class" and it introduces the descriptive phrase *that she took last fall*, which tells us something more about the class.

Interrogative pronouns are the curious cousins of relative pronouns. They're identical to their relative pronoun twins such as "who," "which," and "that," but they're being used to ask a question: *Who took my cake? Which way did he go?*

Pronoun Fact #2: Some Pronouns Have Forms That Vary According to Person and Number

You know this; you just don't know that you know it. Let's start by defining terms—and pay attention, because this person and number stuff comes in handy for discussions on verbs, too—"person" is used in this context to refer to the particular person or thing being spoken of. Personal pronouns are the only type of pronouns with forms that vary according to this idea of person, and there are three possible choices in form. The first-person form is used when you're referring to yourself. Think of the label "first" as reflecting your status as number one in importance (in your own eyes, anyway). "I" is a first-person form. The second-person form is for when you're referring to the person you're addressing—"you" is an example. And the third person refers to the person or thing being spoken about, as in "he," "she," and "it."

Wait a minute, you may be thinking. *You keep saying "person" as though I never talk about more than one person at a time. Why, I've been known to refer to two people at once! In fact, I did it just this morning, when I said, "You kids had better get a move on."* This is where the question of number comes in. Number simply means the number of people being referred to—either one person or thing, in which case the number is singular, or more than one, in which case the number is plural. Personal pronoun forms vary in number, and so do demonstrative pronouns, as noted earlier when we talked about "this" and "these."

When you throw the concepts of person and number together, the resulting line-up for personal pronouns is this:

The first-person singular is I.
The second-person singular is you.
The third-person singular is he, she, or it.

The first-person plural is we.
The second-person plural is you.
The third-person plural is they.

You'll notice that the singular and plural forms for the second person are the same word, "you." Nobody said these things always made sense.

36

Pronoun Fact #3: Personal Pronoun Forms Also Vary According to Case

We said earlier that the general role of a personal pronoun in a sentence is to stand in for a particular person or thing. Well, the "case" form of that personal pronoun gets a lot more specific by indicating exactly how that pronoun relates to the other words in the sentence. The three cases are the nominative case, which is sometimes called the subjective case; the objective case; and the possessive case. Getting a grip on this concept of case requires some background on the parts of a sentence, which we won't cover until the second section of this review. So rather than burning up all your circuits with a detailed talk on cases here, we'll cover this important topic in a separate lesson in Chapter 1.

#3: The Verb: Tense, Voice, and Mood

Verbs describe an action or a state of being. Their role is to make a statement about the subject of your sentence, that is, about whomever or whatever you're talking. When we refer to a verb describing an *action*, we mean this in its broadest sense, including not only physical actions such as "run," "grow," or "squeeze," but also nonphysical actions such as "hope," "solve," and "need." Any word describing what the subject of the sentence is doing is an action verb. For example:

Kim <u>ran</u> to the door.
Steve often <u>thinks</u> about Mary.
Tracy <u>embarrassed</u> herself at the party.

But often the subject of the sentence isn't doing something, it simply *is* something, such as hungry or female or in line for a promotion. Verbs that express a state of being are called linking verbs, because they link the subject of the sentence to the description of the state or condition that the subject is in. The most common linking verb by far is the verb "to be," which

37

includes the forms "am," "is," "are," "was," "were," "have been," "had been," "will be," "will have been," and others. Here are some sentences featuring the linking verb "to be":

The ambassador is a woman.
John will be the next vice president.
Dave was tired.

And here are a few examples of other linking verbs at work. You'll notice that some of these, such as the verbs "look" and "taste," can also be action verbs in other contexts:

Hot dogs taste better with mustard.
Terry remained unhappy.
Joan looks incredibly healthy.

The verb's role of expressing action or a state of being is just the tip of the iceberg, however. Verbs are the most powerful part of speech because they not only tell you the nature of the action itself, but also provide other important information about that action. The benevolent verb offers us three manners of description, and these are tense, voice, and mood.

The **tense** form of a verb tells us when the action occurred or will occur. For example, *he will jump* tells us that the jumping action will occur in the future, whereas *he jumped* tells us it occurred in the past. Tense forms represent the largest minefield in verb country—the cause of all kinds of errors. The first lesson in Chapter 1 provides a look at tenses in greater depth.

The **voice** of a verb tells something about the relationship between the action of the verb and the subject of the sentence— the person or thing the sentence is about. The **active voice** is used to show that the subject is doing the acting, as in *John leads the group*. The **passive voice** is used to show that the subject is on the receiving end of the action, as in *John is led by the group*.

The **mood** of a verb tells us in what manner the verb is communicating the action. When we make basic statements or ask questions, we use the **indicative mood**, as in *I leave at 5* and *Are you taking the car?* The indicative mood is the one we use most often. The **imperative mood** is used to make a request or a command, as in *Get in here right now* or *Bring me a resume*. The **subjunctive mood** is used to express a hypothetical situation or a condition in opposition to the facts and sometimes to express a wish. It is most often used with the verb "to be" in sentences or phrases beginning with "if." For example, *If Jane were home, things would be different* and *I wish I were rich*. The subjunctive mood is not called for often, but when it is, it can be a troublemaker. See the end of Chapter 1 for help in correcting the most common error made with the subjunctive mood.

#4: The Adjective

Adjectives are words that modify nouns and pronouns. That is, they alter slightly the meaning of the noun or pronoun, either by describing something about it or by limiting its meaning to a more definite item or number. In the phrases *red hair*, *swollen feet*, and *unpredictable temper*, the adjectives "red," "swollen," and "unpredictable" have modified the nouns "hair," "feet," and "temper" by describing a characteristic of each.

It's easy to think of adjectives only as descriptive words. But then you'd be missing half the fun—adjectives have more personality than that. So let's have a word about nouns and pronouns functioning as adjectives and also about the articles "a," "an," and "the."

Nouns Functioning as Adjectives

Nouns aren't satisfied to just stay at home and name things. They go out dressed as adjectives all the time. For example, the word "paper" is a noun. But in the phrase *paper airplane*, the word "paper" is being used as an adjective modifying the noun "airplane"—it tells us what *kind* of airplane we're dealing with. Similarly, in the phrase *airplane mechanic*, the noun "airplane" is now being used as an adjective to describe the noun "mechanic."

Pronouns Functioning as Adjectives

Like nouns, pronouns are commonly used as adjectives—a pronoun such as "my" before a noun modifies the noun by telling you who it belongs to. Here are a few phrases in which pronouns function as adjectives:

Our house in Baltimore
Her candy
Take either suit
My sister
Exercise each week

The Articles: "A," "An," and "The"

These three go-everywhere, do-everything words are considered adjectives too, even though they have their own name, *articles*. If this seems confusing, think of how they function: they tell us something more about the noun they're in front of. For example, "a" and "an" are called indefinite articles, because they refer to *any* single member of the group named by the noun, but not to a particular or definite member. In the phrases *a headache* and *an elephant*, we mean any member of the classes of headaches and elephants. On the other hand, the definite article "the" refers to a specific, definite member of some group. Saying *the office* instead of *an office* indicates that we have in mind a particular office and not just any old place of business.

#5: The Adverb

Like adjectives, adverbs are modifiers: They define or limit the meaning of other words. But unlike adjectives, which can only modify nouns or pronouns, adverbs have a kind of prima donna complex. They leave nouns and pronouns alone, but they feel they have something important to say about nearly everybody else—modifying verbs, adjectives, and each other. Let's look first at the different jobs the adverb can do.

As the name suggests, the most common role of the adverb is to modify the meaning of a verb, usually by answering the questions where, when, how, or to what extent. For example, in the phrase, *leave quickly*, "leave" is the verb, and the adverb "quickly" describes the manner in which the action of leaving is carried out. A few more examples: *Look longingly*, *answer abruptly*, *move forward*, *stop immediately*, *sometimes play*, *nearly finish*, *always love*.

Adverbs can also modify adjectives, as in the phrase *nearly complete painting*. Here, the noun "painting" is modified by the adjective "complete" and the adjective "complete" is modified by the adverb "nearly," giving us the full meaning that the painting is almost, but not quite, finished. Here are a few more examples of adverbs modifying adjectives:

Virtually impassable road
(The adverb "virtually" modifies "impassable.")
Almost a year
(The adverb "almost" modifies "a.")
Precisely 10 yards
(The adverb "precisely" modifies "10.")
Slightly frayed collar
(The adverb "slightly" modifies "frayed.")
Evenly spaced items
(The adverb "evenly" modifies "spaced.")

Adverbs also have little love fests in which they modify each other, as in the sentence, *The players were almost evenly matched.* Here, the verb *matched* is modified by the adverb, *evenly.* Then the adverb *evenly* is itself modified in turn by another adverb, *almost*, giving us the meaning that the players are fairly close, but not completely equal, in skill level. A few more examples of adverbs modifying adverbs:

> She was <u>somewhat</u> rudely interrupted.
> (The adverb "somewhat" modifies "rudely.")
> I left <u>rather</u> quickly.
> (The adverb "rather" modifies "quickly.")
> Bob is <u>always</u> extremely funny.
> (The adverb "always" modifies "extremely.")

A word about adverb forms: You'll notice from the preceding examples that while many adverbs such as "evenly" and "precisely" have "-ly" endings, others, such as "somewhat" and "rather" do not. A large group of adverbs fall into the latter category, including—to name only a few—words such as "again," "late," "little," "there," "often," "when," "where," "why," "how," "too," and "much." Here are a few examples of these adverbs at work:

> He came <u>late</u> to the party.
> (The adverb "late" modifies the verb "came.")
> I went home <u>again</u>.
> (The adverb "again" modifies the verb "went.")
> Deborah wears <u>too</u> many necklaces.
> (The adverb "too" modifies the adjective "many.")

In summary, there's no shortcut such as "-ly" endings or position within the sentence to tell you for certain that a word is an adverb. The only way to know for sure is to figure out if it's modifying the meaning of a verb, an adjective, or another adverb. If it's modifying a noun or a pronoun, you've got yourself an adjective instead.

42

#6: The Preposition

Prepositions are a piece of cake. They are simply words used to show a relationship between a noun or a pronoun and certain other words in your sentence. And the easy way to remember this is to think of the word "position" contained within "preposition"—as in the position of one thing relative to another. In the sentence *Harry drank himself under the table*, "under" is the preposition. It shows the relationship between the unwise "Harry" (a noun) and "table" (another noun). Other common prepositions include "above," "after," "around," "at," "before," "below," "between," "by," "during," "except," "from," and "within."

There is also such a thing as a compound preposition, which serves exactly the same purpose of expressing a relationship between two things, but which is made up of more than one word, such as "according to," "because of," and "instead of."

Here's a great illustration of how different prepositions can express different relationships between the same sets of words. Watch how the meaning changes if we begin with the preposition *across* and then substitute others within the same sentence:

They traveled <u>across</u> the forest.
They traveled <u>around</u> the forest.
They traveled <u>beyond</u> the forest.
They traveled <u>into</u> the forest.
They traveled <u>near</u> the forest.
They traveled <u>toward</u> the forest.
They traveled <u>out</u> of the forest.

It's also important to remember, as we've noted throughout, that some words function as more than one part of speech. Prepositions are no exception. The word *outside*, for example, can be a noun, as in *She wrote his name on the <u>outside</u> of the package*; a preposition, as in *Please clean that engine*

43

outside the house; or an adjective, as in *There's an* <u>outside</u> *chance your umbrella will turn up in the lost and found.*

#7: The Conjunction—
Coordinating and Subordinating

Conjunctions are words that join other words and phrases together, just as the back end of the term con*junction* suggests. (Think of the junction of two freeways.) There are coordinating conjunctions such as "and," "or," "nor," "but," "for," "yet," and "so," and subordinating conjunctions such as "because," "when," "if," "though," "unless," "until," and "whether."

Coordinating Conjunctions

Coordinating conjunctions connect words and phrases that have equal grammatical status. This means nouns with nouns, adjectives with adjectives, and pairs of phrases designed to carry equal weight within the sentence. For example:

They brought food <u>and</u> clothes.
(The conjunction "and" joins two nouns, "food" and "clothes.")
The bathroom was old <u>but</u> clean.
(The conjunction "but" joins two adjectives, "old" and "clean.")
He ran <u>or</u> bicycled every day.
(The conjunction "or" joins two verbs, "ran" and "bicycled.")
The cat ran across the room <u>and</u> under the couch.
(The conjunction "and" joins the two equally important phrases, "across the room" and "under the couch.")

Most coordinating conjunctions are made up of one word, such as *and* or *but* in the previous examples. But sometimes coordinating conjunctions have two parts, which work in tandem to join comparable words and phrases together. Examples of these are "either/or," "both/and," and "not only/but also," sometimes shortened to "not only/but." Here's how they work in a sentence:

> He ate <u>both</u> the cake <u>and</u> the ice cream.
> (The conjunction "both/and" joins two nouns, "cake" and "ice cream.")
> She's <u>not only</u> glamorous <u>but</u> strong.
> (The conjunction "not only/but" joins two adjectives, "glamorous" and "strong.")
> It's <u>either</u> on the stove <u>or</u> in the oven.
> (The conjunction "either/or" joins two comparable phrases, "on the stove" and "in the oven.")

Subordinating Conjunctions

Unlike coordinating conjunctions, subordinating conjunctions join together parts of a sentence that *aren't* on equal grammatical footing. Instead, within the world of that sentence, one of the parts depends upon the other for its meaning and is therefore lower in rank or importance—it's *subordinate* to the other. For example, in the sentence *He couldn't go to school because he was sick*, "because" is the subordinating conjunction. It introduces the subordinate clause, "because he was sick," which cannot stand on its own as a sentence but instead depends upon the main portion of the sentence, "he couldn't go to school," for its meaning. The following are some more examples of subordinating conjunctions at work. Note two things: First, the phrases they introduce aren't always at the back end of the sentence; second, many of these conjunctions can also function as other parts of speech such as adverbs and prepositions.

> <u>Since</u> your car is in the shop, let us drive.
> We can leave <u>when</u> Stan arrives.
> Jane doesn't know <u>whether</u> she'll attend the party.
> <u>If</u> you take that, you'll be sorry.

45

<u>As</u> I told him before, John's always welcome here.
Laura won't take the job <u>unless</u> the salary is good.

#8: The Interjection!

Interjections are words thrown into a sentence to express excitement and intensity in actions or emotion. Common interjections are "Hey!" "Wow!" "Oh no!" and "Great!" Most of these words function in other parts of speech, but when they are used as interjections, they stand alone.

Now that you've got your feet wet with the eight parts of speech, it's time to wade all the way into the water and master the basic parts of a sentence. And that's just what the next section will help you do.

The Parts of a Sentence

There is enough detailed terminology floating around on the parts of the sentence to make your head spin. But we'll just focus here on the basic four: subjects, predicates, clauses, and complements. Before we launch into those, however, let's make sure we're straight on the precise definition of a sentence.

Sentences vs. Sentence Fragments

You can't just string together any set of words and punctuation marks you like and call it a sentence—the selection committee for this club is a little more picky than that. In order to qualify, the group of words must express a complete thought.

> A **sentence** must identify what or whom you're talking about and it must say something about that person, thing, or abstract concept.

Without identification and explanation, you've got yourself a fragment, a bit, a piece, a parcel—but no sentence. Here are a couple of fragments:

Ran to the front door.
(This group of words isn't a sentence because it doesn't tell us who it was that did the running.)
David and Elizabeth's daughter, Kelly.
(This is a fragment because we know who we're talking about, but we're not saying anything about her.)

If we said *Kelly ran to the door*, however, we would have a complete sentence, including both an identification of whom we're talking about and a statement about her. These two parts are known as the subject and the predicate, the basic foundation of the sentence.

A Close-up Look at Subjects and Predicates

> The **subject** is the who or the what that a sentence is all about.

The subject might be one word, such as "he," but it might also be a group of words, such as "the sweater he got for Christmas" or "the idea that he would get yet another sweater next Christmas." Here is an example of each of these subjects in a sentence:

He got a sweater for Christmas.
The sweater he got for Christmas was too small for him.
The idea that he would get yet another sweater next Christmas frustrated him.

Do you see that although the pronoun "he" and the noun "sweater" are involved in all three sentences, the subject changes from one to the other? The first sentence is about a person, and what we learn about him is that he got a sweater. The second sentence is about a thing, the sweater he got for Christmas, and the fact that it was too small. The third sentence is about an abstract concept, the idea of getting another

47

sweater, and the fact that it was bound to frustrate the unfortunate person who would receive it.

> The **predicate** is the part of the sentence with the verb in it.

The predicate is composed of every other word in the sentence that's not the subject. As with the subject, this might be only one word, the verb, or it might be a whole group of words. If the sentence is *I will go to Austria as soon as the rates get better*, the subject, as you probably guessed, is "I," and the predicate is everything else—"will go to Austria as soon as the rates get better." Let's identify the subject and predicate in a few more sentences:

He jogs.
(The subject is "he," the predicate is "jogs.")
Dana's father went into the hospital yesterday.
(The subject is "Dana's father," the predicate is "went into the hospital yesterday.")
The television in the den doesn't work.
(The subject is "the television in the den," the predicate is "doesn't work.")

Notice that every single word in the sentence belongs to either the subject or the predicate—once those two parts are identified, there aren't any words left over. You'll also notice that while the subject always contains a noun or a pronoun, it can also have other descriptive words—adjectives, prepositions, etc.—surrounding that noun or pronoun. "The television in the den" is the *complete subject* in the last sentence. The *simple subject* is the noun "television."

Those same concepts of "simple" and "complete" apply to predicates. In the sentence *Dana's father went into the hospital yesterday*, the complete predicate is "went into the hospital yesterday," but the simple predicate is the verb, "went."

Complements

We explained earlier that all sentences need to express a complete thought. We also said they need a subject and a verb in order to do that. And we didn't lie. But we didn't tell the whole truth either, and that's where complements come in.

> A **complement** is the part of the predicate that completes the meaning of the verb.

Some verbs need a little help before the sentence they're in can express a complete thought. And other verbs may not require this help, but you want to provide it anyway in order to express your meaning more precisely. For example, take the verb "take." If you say *she takes*, you have both a subject and a verb, but hardly a complete thought. What is it that she's taking? You need a complement, for example, *piano lessons*. The sentence *She takes piano lessons* expresses a complete thought.

There are three types of complements: direct objects, indirect objects, and complements of linking verbs. Don't worry if this sounds overwhelming—it's actually fairly simple once you get the hang of it. Let's look first at direct objects.

Direct Objects

Direct objects complete the meaning of verbs expressing action by telling you what or whom is on the receiving end of it. In the previous example, *she takes piano lessons*, "take" is an action verb and "piano lessons" is a direct object. See if you can identify the direct objects in these sentences:

Jack set the table.
(The direct object of "set" is "table.")
That diet used up all my willpower.
(The direct object of "used" is "willpower." Note that the object doesn't always have to be a tangible object.)

49

The burglars stole her cash and jewelry.
(The direct objects of "stole" are "cash" and "jewelry."
Yes, this means there can be more than one direct object
at a time.)

Indirect Objects

Indirect objects are also used as complements of action
verbs, but they differ from direct objects in a couple of ways.
First, they're almost never used on their own; they usually precede a direct object. Second, rather than answering the questions *what* or *whom*, indirect objects answer the questions *to
whom* or *for whom*. In the sentence *Can you hand me that
wrench?* the indirect object is "me" and the direct object is
"wrench." "Wrench" answers the question *what* was handed,
and "me" answers the question *to whom* it was handed. Practice picking out the direct and indirect objects in these sentences:

Pay him 70,000 dollars for the first year.
(What was paid? The direct object is "dollars." To whom
was it paid? The indirect object is "him.")
Her mother bought her the most awful dress.
(What was bought? The direct object is "dress." For whom
was it bought? The indirect object is "her.")

Complements of Linking Verbs

Linking verbs don't express action, but simply "link" (as
their name suggests) the subject of the sentence to the complement, which modifies or describes the subject. The most common linking verb is "to be" (for the forms of the verb "to be"
see pages 89-90).

He was the strangest person she had ever met.
(Here the linking verb "was" links the subject "he" to the
complement "the strangest person she had ever met.")

50

Why have a special category for the complements of linking verbs? Well, when you've got a pronoun in the complement of a sentence, it's important to know whether you've got an action verb or a linking verb, because these verbs require different pronouns. All that the complement of a linking verb can do is to describe the subject, so it has the same grammatical form that a subject would, as in the following sentence:

It was she who accidentally sat on your painting this morning.

Here the linking verb "was" links the subject "it" with the complement "she." If the verb were an action verb, it would be followed by "her" as either the direct object (*I saw her at the store yesterday*) or the indirect object (*I gave her the cheese log*). But because we've got a linking verb, we need the same kind of pronoun in the complement that we would use in the subject position, and that's "she." You'll have plenty of opportunities to practice with this kind of sentence in Chapter 1.

Clauses—Independent and Subordinate

Grab hold of something to hang on to while we discuss clauses, because we're going to add another layer of complexity.

> A **clause** is a group of words that contains a subject and a predicate and is located within a sentence.

You may be thinking that this sounds awfully much like the definition of a sentence: subject plus predicate. But the key words here are "located within a sentence." Sentences can have two or more clauses, each containing its own subject and predicate. Think of it as the difference between a single-family home and an apartment building. The separate house has all the basic elements required in a home together under one roof—kitchen, bedrooms, etc. The apartment building contains more than one unit, or home, each with the same set of basic elements, but those units don't stand alone, they're together under one roof. A sentence can be like the house, with just one basic subject and predicate, or it can be like the apartment building, full of units, or clauses, each with its own subject and predicate. Here is an example of a sentences with more than one clause:

> We tickled his feet, and he begged for mercy.

There are two clauses here. One is "we tickled his feet," where the subject is "we," and the predicate is "tickled his feet." The other clause is "he begged for mercy," and there the subject is "he," and the predicate is "begged for mercy." This type of clause is called an independent clause.

> An **independent clause** is a clause that can stand on its own as a sentence because it doesn't depend on anything else for its meaning.

Here are two more sentences featuring independent clauses. See if you can identify them before we jump in with the answer:

> Joe is interested in nothing but himself, and this makes him incredibly boring to talk to.
> (Clause #1: "Joe is interested in nothing but himself." The subject is "Joe" and the predicate is "is interested in nothing but himself." Clause #2: "This makes him incredibly boring to talk to." The subject is "this" and the predicate is "makes him incredibly boring to talk to.")
> None of the guests liked the host, but they all enjoyed themselves at the party.
> (Clause #1: "None of the guests liked the host." The subject is "none of the guests," and the predicate is "liked the host." Clause #2: "They all enjoyed themselves at the party." The subject is "they all" and the predicate is "enjoyed themselves at the party.")

Note that in all these cases, you could have used any of these clauses as a sentence on its own. For example, "None of the guests liked the host. They all enjoyed themselves at the party."

The second basic type of clause is the subordinate clause, and its nature is to be clingy. (It is sometimes called the dependent clause.) It can't end the relationship with the main clause in the sentence, because it knows it doesn't have what it takes to go off on its own.

> A **subordinate clause** is one that cannot stand on its own as a sentence because it depends on something in the main clause for its meaning.

A subordinate clause doesn't contain the main idea of the sentence as a whole, even though it contains a subject and a predicate. Instead, it's as though all the words in the clause sign a contract agreeing to function as one of three parts of speech, an adjective, an adverb, or a noun, as a means of providing more information about something in the main clause. Here's an example of each type.

Adjective Clause: *I* only pretended to read the copy of *War and Peace* that I brought to the beach.

The main clause is "I only pretended to read the copy of *War and Peace*." The subordinate adjective clause is "that I brought to the beach." Do you see how this couldn't stand on its own as a sentence? In this clause, the subject is "I," and the predicate is "brought to the beach." The whole clause as a unit modifies the noun "copy" in the main clause by telling us more about it.

Adverbial Clause: She turns heads because she wears too much perfume.

The main clause is "she turns heads." The subordinate adverbial clause is "because she wears too much perfume." This clause modifies the verb "turns" in the main clause by telling us why the turning happens.

Noun Clause: Alexandra Margaret May Whitinghill Smyth's problem is that she has too many names for one person.

The subordinate noun clause here is "that she has too many names for one person." The subject of the noun clause is "she," the predicate is "has too many names for one person," and the whole clause functions as a noun by naming what the problem is.

Congratulations, you've graduated from grammar school. You now have enough basic information to get the most out of the program that follows and to bore your friends at parties with your knowledge of the mechanics of grammar. We recommend that you go over this review a few times to really get the concepts and the terminology down pat. And if you ever have a question when you're going through the chapters ahead, remember that you have a friend in the Grammar Review. So if you have to look up "subordinate clause" four or five times as you work through the program, don't worry. We won't tell.

Perplexing Pronouns

CHAPTER 1

It's easy to explain what a pronoun is: It's a word used in place of a noun. Saying, "She ran away," when you mean your cat, is an example of a pronoun in action. But using pronouns correctly can be tricky, because they come in different types, and some of these types come in a variety of forms, so that before you know it, you can't even explain where you've been all day. Is it, "Joe invited Bill and me to play golf"? Or "Bill and I"?

In this chapter, we'll focus mainly on three areas of particular difficulty:

❑ First, the **cases** of certain pronouns and how to tell which you should use. This is the "I" vs. "me" and "who" vs. "whom" stuff that gives many of us so much trouble.

❑ Second, the two **relative pronouns** "which" and "that" and how to choose between them.

❑ And third, the overly popular **intensive** or **reflexive** pronouns, such as "myself" or "himself," and how to avoid putting them where they don't belong.

A Lesson on Pronoun Cases

Personal pronouns and a couple of relative pronouns vary in form according to person and number (as discussed in the Grammar Review) and according to case as well. The three cases are the subjective case (sometimes called the nominative case), the objective case, and the possessive case. You choose between them according to the role you're asking the pronoun to take on in a sentence.

For a basic illustration, let's say you're referring to yourself and your ownership of a book. You might say *I own that book* or *That book belongs to me* or *That book is mine*. In those three sentences we used the first-person singular pronouns "I," "me," and "mine." In each instance, of course, you're referring to yourself, but the form of the pronoun you use to do it changes. In the first sentence, *I own that book*, you are the subject of the sentence and identified by the pronoun "I." "I" is the subjective case. In the second sentence, *That book belongs to me*, the subject is "that book," and you, the owner, are now the object of the preposition "to," and you're identified by the pronoun "me." "Me" is the objective case. And in the third sentence, *That book is mine*, you, the owner, have an adjectival role indicated by the pronoun "mine." "Mine" is the possessive case.

Here are the case forms for each of the personal pronouns— and the two relative pronouns that take different case forms. The pronouns themselves are familiar, of course, but watch how they sort themselves according to case, and notice that some of the forms do not vary.

Personal Pronoun Case Forms

	Subjective	Objective	Possessive
Personal	I	me	my, mine
Pronouns	you	you	your, yours
	he	him	his
	she	her	her, hers
	it	it	its
	we	us	our, ours
	they	them	their, theirs

Relative Pronoun Case Forms

	Subjective	Objective	Possessive
Relative	who	whom	whose
Pronouns	whoever	whomever	whosever

How do you determine the correct case for a given pronoun? There are a bunch of little rules that cover less common situations, but the basic guidelines are:

Use the subjective case when...

❑ **The pronoun is the subject of the verb.**

In other words, when the pronoun is the person or thing that commits the action.

I, *we*, *you*, *he*, *she*, *it*, *they* ran away.

❑ **The pronoun follows a finite form of the verb "to be" (any form of "to be" except the infinitive form with the "to" in front of it).**

In other words, use the subjective case if the pronoun is the complement of the linking verb "to be" (see the Grammar Review for more on this concept):

They believed that the thief was *I*, *you*, *he*, *she*.
They believed that the thieves were *we*, *you*, *they*.

Use the objective case when...

❏ **The pronoun is the object of a verb.**

The pronoun "receives" the action in the sentence: it isn't doing anything, but something is being done to it:

> The search team found *me, him, her, it, us, you, them*.

❏ **The pronoun is the indirect object of a verb.**

The pronoun is the person or thing for whom (or for which) something is being done:

> Bob gave *me, him, her, us, you, them* all the zucchini in his garden.

❏ **The pronoun is the subject of an infinitive.**

This is different from being the subject of the whole sentence, in which you'd use the subjective case. In the following sentence, "the boss" is the subject of the main verb, "told," but "me" (or one of the other pronoun choices) is the subject of the verb "to do," which is being used in this sentence in its infinitive form, with the "to" in front:

> The boss told *me, him, her, us, you, them* to do it.

❏ **The pronoun is the object of an infinitive.**

This means the pronoun is identifying someone on the receiving end of the action expressed by the infinitive. Remember, the infinitive is not the main verb in this sentence, it's a secondary part of the predicate:

> The judge wanted to believe *me, him, her, it, us, you, them*.

❏ **The pronoun is the object of a preposition.**

> Put the blanket over *me, you, him, her, it, us, them*.

Use the possessive case when...

❏ **The pronoun itself is being used to indicate possession.**

> *My, your, her, his, our, their* toaster.

58

Subjective and Objective Cases

1. I vs. Me

> **Don't Say:** This is a problem for Ellen and *I* to solve.
> **Say Instead:** This is a problem for Ellen and *me* to solve.

Here's Why: Let's apply the rule that pronoun cases are supposed to agree with their roles in the sentence. In this sentence, the subject is the word "this." "Ellen," and "I" are subjects too, but they're subjects of the infinitive "to solve," so "I," the subjective case, is incorrect here.

Almost no one would pick the wrong form of the pronoun in this sentence if there weren't two people involved. You'd say, "this is a problem for me to solve," using the correct objective case instinctively. But throw another person in there, and everybody squirms, thinking "Ellen and me" sounds funny. We're often afraid of the word "me," but "me" is perfectly respectable and hates being shunted aside for no reason.

Tip: Here's an easy way to figure out whether "I" or "me" is correct when there's more than one person in your sentence. Ask yourself what form of the pronoun you'd pick if you took the other person out, just like we did when we dumped poor Ellen. The choice you make between "I" and "me" when there's no one else involved is the same one you should make when everyone and your mother are part of the story. Let's look at a few more examples to cement this down:

Instead of <u>Me</u> and Jerry are leaving, *say* Jerry and I are leaving.

(Here, the personal pronoun is intended to be the subject of the verb "are," so you need the subjective case form, "I." Double-check by using the tip: Would you say, "Me are leaving?" No, you'd say, "I am leaving," so "I" is correct.)

Instead of saying It was me, *say* It was I.

(Remember, you need the subjective case whenever the personal pronoun follows a form of the verb "to be" without the "to" in front, whenever it's the complement of a linking verb. That's what we've got going on here. The verb "was" in this sentence is of course a form of the verb "to be." So we need the subjective pronoun, "I," instead of the objective form, "me.")

Still more examples, all correct:

Jack and Jill are going with me down the hill.
Jack and I are going down the hill with Jill.
There's nothing between Laverne and me, I swear!
Will you come to dinner with Sandy and me?
They've known Larry and me for years.
Larry and I have known them for years.

2. She vs. Her

Don't Say: Yes, this is *her*; who's calling?
Say Instead: Yes, this is *she*; who's calling?

Here's Why: In this sentence, the pronoun follows a finite form of the verb "to be," namely "is." That means the subjective case, "she," is required. Additional correct "she" and "her" examples are:

She, as the oldest, was the most responsible.
Her opinions were ignored by her six elder brothers.
She and I are cooking together.
A nervous look passed between her and him.

"He" and "him" follow the same pattern: use "he" following a finite form of the verb "to be":

This is he.
It was he who we saw dancing with Lucille.

But use "him" as the direct object of a verb, the indirect object of a verb, or the object of a preposition.

We saw <u>him</u> at the dance hall with Lucille.
Lucille was dancing with <u>him</u>.
Lucille gave <u>him</u> a meaningful glance.

3. Who vs. Whom

Don't Say: *Who* is the present for?
Say Instead: *Whom* is the present for?

Here's Why: Think about what role the pronoun is playing here. The subject of this sentence is "the present." The pronoun is an object, the object of the preposition "for," to be exact. So it should be in the objective case, and that's "whom."

Tip: When deciding between "who" and "whom," it can be easier if you use the **"m" test**: Think of how you would restate the sentence with the pronoun he/hi**m** or they/the**m**, and if you use a form that ends in "m," you need "who**m**." For example, in this sentence, you'd say, *Is the present for <u>the**m**</u>?* You wouldn't say, *Is the present for <u>they</u>.* That "the**m**," in the objective case—with the "m" on the end—is your clue that you need the objective case form "who**m**" with the "m" on the end. Or you can figure out how you'd answer a who/who**m** question using he or hi**m**. In the sentence *Who/whom was the friend you brought with you?* you would answer "he is the friend" not "him is the friend." Subjective case, no "m"—that's the signal that "who" is correct.

Here are more correct uses of "who" and "whom":

That's the actor <u>whom</u> Sally adores. (Sally adores him.)
Can I tell her <u>who</u> is calling? (He is calling.)
<u>Whom</u> are you asking to the party? (You are asking them to the party.)

To <u>whom</u> are you returning these roses? (You are returning the roses to him.)
I want the people <u>who</u> did this to step forward. (They did this.)

Now here's a tricky correct example that even "who/whom" whizzes can get confused:

She'll marry the man <u>who</u> she thinks has the finest collection of ties.

The "she thinks" gives a lot of people fits here: It may seem as if the pronoun should be the object of "thinks" and that therefore we need "whom." But the pronoun is actually the subject of "has," which becomes clear when we apply the "m" test. You wouldn't say *She thinks <u>him</u> has the finest collection of ties*, instead, you'd say, *She thinks <u>he</u> has the finest collection of ties*. No "m," so we need "who." Many sentences follow a similar pattern when they include an extra clause reporting what people believe, think, or say.

Sheila, <u>who</u> I believe has the largest collection of fountain pens in North America, always writes letters on her computer.
My blind date, <u>who</u> you'd said would be "interesting," proved to be just that.

4. Whoever vs. Whomever

Don't Say: Give the tickets to *whomever* can use them.
Say Instead: Give the tickets to *whoever* can use them.

Here's Why: You may have been tempted to say "whomever" here, because it may seem to be the object of "to." But actually the object of "to" is the whole final clause "whoever can use them." Within that clause, the pronoun is the subject of the verb "can," so the subjective case is required, and that's "whoever."

Grammatically, "whoever" and "whomever" work the same way that "who" and "whom" do. Wherever you would use "who," you use "whoever," and wherever you would use "whom," you use "whomever." "Whoever" can be used as the subject of a verb, for example:

Whoever took my belt had better give it back.
Whoever said that was crazy.

"Whomever" can put in an appearance as a verb's object:

Please bring whomever you like to the picnic.

But these pronouns get tough when it's hard to tell which part of the sentence determines which pronoun we should use. That's what might happen in the first sample sentence, *Give the tickets to whoever can use them.* More correct examples of this tricky pattern are:

It will be hard for whoever wins to run the state.
("Whoever" is the subject of "wins.")
We'll have to get whomever we can to do the job.
("Whomever" is the subject of the infinitive "to do.")

Test: Subjective and Objective Cases

Please circle the correct choice.

1. It was (I, me) who ate the entire bag of potato chips while you were out.

2. Aunt Dorothy left her collection of wrestling memorabilia to David and (I, me).

3. Between you and (I, me), Angela's grammar leaves a great deal to be desired.

4. Allan was having lunch with Anne and (I, me) when he heard the news.

5. Warren and (I, me) haven't spoken since our argument 10 years ago.

6. They gave Adam and (I, me) heavy-duty umbrellas when we moved to Seattle.

7. He isn't picky; he's dating not only Jill, but also Frederika, Caroline, and (I, me).

8. The agency prizes Carol, (who, whom) can type at least 60 words per minute.

9. These are the people among (who, whom) you will be living next semester.

10. I asked her (who, whom) she meant to marry after she dumped Alfred.

11. The man (who, whom) Gloria thought was the waiter proved to be the company president.

12. The lawyers, (who, whom) we haven't spoken to in months, submitted an itemized bill this morning.

13. The woman (who, whom) he'd said was his wife proved to be his accountant.

14. (Whoever, Whomever) is hiding under the bed had better come out this minute.

15. He'll send candy to (whoever, whomever) he likes best.

16. Cats attach themselves to (whoever, whomever) is allergic to them.

17. They gave a bag of bonbons to (whoever, whomever) showed up at the door.

18. Hubert announced he'd fight (whoever, whomever) took up his challenge.

19. I'll talk to (whoever, whomever) you think I should.

20. (He, him) and (I, me) were hired as short-order cooks, but were promoted to vice presidents in charge of culinary arts.

21. I gave Bill and (she, her) detailed directions, but they still got lost.

22. It is (she, her) who owns the car, but it was (he, him) who crashed it into a tree.

23. Something is going on between (she, her) and (he, him).

24. The bees attacked Karen and (he, him) while they were contemplating the sunset.

25. Have you ever met Julia? This is (she, her).

26. This isn't (he, him); this is his brother. May I ask who's calling?

Answer Key: Subjective and Objective Cases

1. I. Subjective case after the verb "was," a finite form of "to be."

2. me. Indirect object of "left."

3. me. Object of preposition "between."

4. me. Object of preposition "with."

5. I. Subject of the verb "haven't."

6. me. Indirect object of "gave."

7. me. Direct object of "dating."

8. who. Subject of "can."

9. whom. Object of the preposition "among."

10. whom. Object of the verb "marry." If we were using a personal pronoun, we'd say *she meant to marry him* (not "he").

11. who. Subject of the verb "was." *Gloria thought he* (not "him") *was the waiter.*

12. whom. Object of the preposition "to." *We haven't spoken to them* (not "they").

13. who. Subject of the verb "was": *he'd said she* (not "her") *was his wife.*

14. Whoever. Subject of the verb "is hiding."

15. whomever. Direct object of "likes." Note that the pronoun takes its case from the clause in which it plays a grammatical role—and that's not necessarily the first clause in the sentence. Here, the entire second clause, "whomever he

likes best," is the indirect object of "send." But within that clause, "whomever" is the object of "likes"; if we were using a personal pronoun, we'd say *he likes them best.*

16. whoever. Subject of the verb "is." This one's tricky. You might have thought the pronoun was the object of "to," but again, as in 15, it's the entire second clause, "whoever is allergic to them," that's the object of "to." Within that clause, "whoever" is the subject of "is"; if we were using a personal pronoun, we'd say *she is allergic to them.*

17. Whoever. Subject of the verb "showed up." Same principle as 16.

18. whoever. Subject of the verb "took up. " Same principle as 16 and 17.

19. whomever. Object of a second understood "talk to": *I'll talk to whomever you think I should talk to.* This one is also tricky. In this case, "whomever" does not play a part in the clauses that follow it; when we try substituting a personal pronoun such as "he" or "she," there's no place to put it (*He you think I should? You think he should I? You think I should he?*). The only way to substitute a personal pronoun is to put it in the "talk to" clause: *you think I should talk to him.*

20. he, I. Subjects of the verb "were hired."

21. her. Indirect object of the verb "gave."

22. she, he. Subjective case following "is," a finite form of the verb "to be."

23. her, him. Objects of the preposition "between."

24. him. Object of the verb "attacked."

25. she. Subjective case following "is," a finite form of the verb "to be."

26. he. Subjective case following "isn't," a finite form of the verb "to be."

Objective and Possessive Cases

5. His vs. Him

> **Don't Say:** It's a question of *him* being ready on time.
> **Say Instead:** It's a question of *his* being ready on time.

Here's Why: This is a problem of using the objective case where the possessive one is needed. What's being possessed? It doesn't have to be tangible, such as a book. In this example it's a state, the state of "being ready on time." So the possessive form "his" is required. The possessives "my," "her," "their," and "your" can be used the same way, as we'll see in the next error.

6. Their vs. Them

> **Don't Say:** It was the teacher's willingness to consider *them* leaving early that surprised the students most.
> **Say Instead:** It was the teacher's willingness to consider *their* leaving early that surprised the students most.

Here's Why: Again, we need the possessive case here, "their." That's because the pronoun isn't functioning as an object, it's doing the job of an adjective by indicating whose early leaving we're talking about.

Here's another correct example:

Marge objected to their eating during the ceremony.

What's being possessed is an action: Marge objects to eating, but not to all eating; she hasn't started a Society for the Prevention of Eating. So we need a possessive adjective to say whose eating Marge objects to: not to eating in general, but to *their* eating.

But wait, it gets trickier. One reason why these sentences are so tough is that they look like another kind of sentence that needs another kind of pronoun. The following example is correct:

Marge saw <u>them</u> eating during the ceremony.

What happened? Well, our emphasis has changed from the action of eating to the people doing the eating. Marge sees *them*—the direct object of the sentence—and "eating" modifies "them"—it describes what they are doing while Marge happens to see them.

Tip: How can you tell which kind of a sentence you've got? One good test is to try leaving the "-ing" word out. If the sentence still communicates the most important part of its meaning, then the emphasis is on the people, and you need the objective case. "Marge saw them" tells us who it was that Marge saw perfectly well; we don't really need to know that they were eating.

But if the meaning of the sentence changes dramatically when you leave out the "-ing" word, then the emphasis is on the action, and all you need is a possessive pronoun to modify it. "Marge objected to them," for example, just doesn't communicate the essence of Marge's original objection. She didn't object to everything about them, to their hair or their clothes or their politics, for example. She objected only to their eating. The emphasis is on the action, so Marge needs a possessive. Here are some more preferred choices of each kind of sentence.

Bob was irritated by <u>my</u> singing in the shower.
We've decided to put a stop to <u>your</u> bickering with your sister.

Because the pronoun depends on what the speaker wants to emphasize, sometimes there is no cut-and-dried "correct" choice: it's entirely up to the speaker. The following two examples are both correct.

Everyone in the house heard <u>me</u> singing in the shower.
Everyone in the house heard <u>my</u> singing in the shower.

Test: Objective and Possessive Cases

Please circle the correct choice.

1. The neighbors wanted to discuss the delicate subject of (him, his) keeping 12 bulldogs in a studio apartment.

2. I've been kept awake all week by (you, your) tromping in and out at all hours of the night.

3. Mother will never approve of (me, my) dating Igor.

4. Mark was irritated by (them, their) assuming they could borrow his wet suit whenever they pleased.

5. Her inability to imagine (him, his) leaving kept her from wondering about (him, his) buying all those suitcases.

6. Petula fails to admire (you, your), surprising though that may be.

7. He found (me, my) eating his sandwich.

8. He objected vigorously to (me, my) eating his sandwich.

9. He insisted that (me, my) eating his sandwich was more impolite than (him, his) spying on me.

10. I had just come home when I discovered (you, your) arriving at my doorstep.

11. The worst thing that ever happened to me was (you, your) arriving at my doorstep.

12. In the forest at midnight, she saw (them, their) dancing about the cauldron and cackling gleefully.

13. She was puzzled by (them, their) cackling gleefully, but she was terrified by (them, their) dancing around the cauldron.

Answer Key: Objective and Possessive Cases

1. his. Possessive pronoun modifying "keeping," which is the object of "of." The neighbors object not to him in general, but to the action of keeping bulldogs.

2. your. Possessive pronoun modifying "tromping," which is the object of "by."

3. my. Possessive pronoun modifying "dating," which is the object of "approve of."

4. their. Possessive pronoun modifying "assuming," which is the object of "by."

5. his, his. Possessive pronouns modifying "leaving" and "buying," which are the objects of "imagine" and "about"

6. you. This is something of a trick question; it's got nothing to do with the errors we've been discussing in this section. We just threw it into remind you of another common "-ing" construction. "You" is the object of the verb "admire"; "surprising," despite its unusual position, is not the object of "admire." Petula does not fail to admire "surprising," she fails to admire "you." Grammatically, "surprising" is the predicate complement of "may be" in the clause "though that may be surprising."

7. me. Object of the verb "found"; "eating" describes "me."

8. my. Possessive modifying eating, which is the object of "object to." He doesn't object to everything about me, or to me in general, but only to the action I am performing: my eating his sandwich.

9. my, his. Possessives modifying eating and spying. In both cases, the action rather than the person is being objected to, so "eating" and "spying" are the direct objects, and the pronouns are possessives modifying them.

10. you. Object of "discovered." I've discovered you, the person, not the action of arriving.

11. your. Possessive modifying "arriving." The worst thing that ever happened to me is not you in general, but the action of arriving. "Arriving" is thus the object of "was," and "your" modifies "arriving."

12. them. Object of the verb "saw."

13. their, their. Possessives modifying "cackling" and "dancing"; in both cases it's the action to which she is reacting.

Relative Pronouns:
"Which," "That," and "Who/Whom"

You should be glad to know that the most important thing about using these pronouns is also the easiest to understand. In fact, you probably are entirely aware of it already, for it's simply a rule that "which" can only be used to refer to *things* (whether they're tangible such as beds or buildings, or intangible such as ideas), but *not to people*. You'd never say, *The plumber which you met yesterday goes to our church*, although you certainly could say, *The plumber goes to our church, which is on the next block*." Because the plumber is a person, the clause describing him needs the pronoun in "the plumber *that* you met..." or "the plumber whom you met...."

There's also a second, trickier rule involving the difference between "which" and "that." To be honest, you're not likely to get into much trouble by neglecting this rule; it's sometimes disregarded by people whose English is otherwise very good, but it *is* a rule that makes sense and that's observed by most careful speakers and writers. Explaining it calls for a bit of specialist's language, but examples should make things pretty clear.

Accordingly, let's consider two sentences. Each of them uses the relative pronoun correctly, and we'll shortly understand why this is the case.

> The cat, <u>which</u> had been sleeping for hours, woke up when the canary sang.
> The cat <u>that</u> had been sleeping for hours was hungrier than the cat that ate the canary.

Now, in the first sentence, the clause "which had been sleeping for hours" gives us some information about the cat, but it isn't essential to the meaning of the sentence; we know the significant fact, that the cat awoke, whether or not we have the additional information contained in the clause, "which had

71

been sleeping." This clause is, we can say, nonessential, or, as the grammarians put it, a **nonrestrictive** clause—nonrestrictive because, although it does describe what the cat has been doing, it doesn't restrict or limit the meaning of the principal clause; the cat awoke, regardless of how long it had been sleeping. Because our clause is thus **nonrestrictive**, or nonessential, we indicate its "expendable" nature by using the pronoun "which" and, in writing, by setting off the clause with commas.

In the second sentence, on the other hand, the clauses beginning with "that" are clearly essential to the meaning of the sentence, which would otherwise only tell us that one (unspecified) cat was hungrier than another (unspecified) cat. For the sentence to do any sort of job, it must narrow its meaning down; it must distinguish between cats, between the sleeper and the canary-eater, and thus *restrict* the principal action to two particular, clearly different creatures. These **restrictive** clauses are not expendable; they are essential to and inseparable from the basic meaning of the sentence. They are signaled by the pronoun "that," and, in writing, they are not set off by commas.

As you can see, the rules can be pretty clearly stated:

> Use **which** in a **nonrestrictive** clause (a clause not essential to the meaning of the sentence).
> Use **that** in a **restrictive** clause (a clause essential to the meaning of the sentence).

There's one pretty obvious exception to these rules. If you have a nonrestrictive clause (calling for "which") but you are referring to a *person*, follow the earlier rule (and probably your own instinct); avoid the "which" and go back to "who" or "whom." So it's proper (and certainly natural) to say:

> Bob, who (and not, in this case, "which") had been spending his day fishing, ate all the hot dogs.

72

With a restrictive clause referring to a person, you can, as with all restrictive clauses, use "that," or, as many people prefer, "who" or "whom." Here are a few examples:

The man that you just insulted is my brother-in-law.
Or: The man <u>whom</u> you just insulted is my brother-in-law.

7. Which vs. That

Don't Say: The invitations *which* we sent by carrier pigeon arrived sooner than the invitations *which* we sent in the mail.
Say Instead: The invitations *that* we sent by carrier pigeon arrived sooner than the invitations *that* we sent in the mail.

Here's Why: In this case "that" is correct, because the clauses are restrictive: They help us distinguish one group of invitations from another group. Here are additional correct examples featuring "which" and "that":

Is she the one <u>that</u> you broke up with?
The tennis ball <u>that</u> the dog played with was wet.
Sharon is the one <u>that</u> I'm going to marry.
The car, <u>which</u> had been stolen only an hour before, was found stripped down to its frame.

Test: Relative Pronouns

Please circle the correct choice.

1. The man next door, (that, which, who, whom) was usually quite a nice person, had been practicing his trombone for hours.

2. His trombone, (that, which, who, whom) he had bought for 50 cents at a flea market, could play only two different notes.

3. The trombone (that, which, who, whom) he'd bought for 50 cents was far better, however, than the trombone (that, which, who, whom) he'd found lying in the alley.

4. The argument (that, which, who, whom) we had about philosophy was far more violent than the argument (that, which, who, whom) we had about baseball.

5. Our dispute, (that, which, who, whom) continued into the small hours of the morning, concerned the fondue pot (that, which) Alison had borrowed and never returned.

6. The man (that, which, who, whom) I marry must be able to make a decent omelette.

7. The woman (that, which, who, whom) hurtled past my airplane window proved to be a skydiver.

8. Her silverware, (that, which) was engraved with the family monogram, included soup spoons the size of small platters.

Answer Key: Relative Pronouns

1. who. Nonrestrictive clause referring to a person (man). Remember, you can't use "which" for a person, and you can't use "that" for a nonrestrictive clause, so "who" is the only possible choice here.

2. which. Nonrestrictive clause referring to a thing (trombone).

3. that, that. Both pronouns are in restrictive clauses (distinguishing which trombone) referring to a thing (trombone).

4. that, that. Both pronouns are in restrictive clauses (distinguishing which argument) referring to a thing (argument).

5. which, that. The first clause is nonrestrictive; it provides unessential information about the length of the argument, so "which" is appropriate. The second clause, however, is restrictive; we need the information it provides in order to know which fondue pot was involved in the dispute; thus, "that" is appropriate in the second clause.

6. that *or* whom. Restrictive clause referring to a person, object of "marry." If the pronoun referred to a thing, it could only be "that," (for example, "the robot that I marry"), but you may use either "that" or "who/whom" to refer to a particular person in a restrictive clause.

7. that *or* who. Restrictive clause providing essential information referring to a person, subject of "hurtled."

8. which. Nonrestrictive clause referring to a thing.

Intensive or Reflexive Pronouns—What They're for and Where NOT to Put Them

Intensive or reflexive refers to a single group of pronouns that people often sprinkle around where they're not needed: "myself," "yourself," "himself," "herself," "itself," "ourselves," "yourselves," and "themselves." The labels **intensive** and **reflexive** are handy because they refer to the only situations in which these pronouns can be correctly used.

❑ **Intensive** usage is just like it sounds: adding emphasis, or intensity, to the subject as a way to reinforce the idea that it's that person who's involved and not someone else. For example:

> You <u>yourself</u> should go there.
> I will keep it <u>myself.</u>
> The mountain <u>itself</u> caused his fall.

❑ **Reflexive** usage is when the pronoun reflects the action of the verb back onto the subject. Think of it as one greedy person or thing who's playing the role of both subject and object in the sentence. For example:

> I hit <u>myself</u> in the knee.
> She warned <u>herself</u> not to do it.
> The garden renewed <u>itself</u> every spring.

The basic rule with intensive and reflective pronouns is that they can ONLY be used in these intensive and reflexive

75

situations. They cannot be used where an ordinary pronoun, such as "I," "me," "she," or "it," would do the job.

Let's look at some errors that people make with these pronouns.

8. Me vs. Myself

> **Don't Say:** Thank you for inviting Jack and *myself*.
> **Say Instead:** Thank you for inviting Jack and *me*.

Here's Why: The pronoun "myself" is not attached in any way to the subject of the sentence here, which is "you," and that's a sign of trouble. It's not intensifying the subject or reflecting the action of the verb "inviting" back onto the subject. So the penalty flag is down. Substituting "myself" when the personal pronoun "me" will suffice occurs a lot when people think that "me" sounds funny or that "myself" sounds more elegant and formal. Don't give in to temptation.

Mnemonic Tip: If a personal pronoun such as "me" or "I" gets the idea across, even if it sounds funny, use it. It'll be correct.

Test: Intensive and Reflexive Pronouns

Please circle the correct choice.

1. We've sent engraved invitations to Connie, Lucille, and (you, yourself).

2. Joe-Bob is bringing corn dogs and beer; caviar will be provided by Charles and (I, me, myself).

3. My wife and (I, me, myself) would be delighted to attend the reception on your yacht.

4. Carolyn and (you, yourself) can come early and stay late.

5. There was no one in the castle but Esmerelda and (I, me, myself).

6. Bonuses were given this year only to Wallace and (I, me, myself).

7. We're calling to confirm that your husband and (you, yourself) have reserved seating at our Annual Bingo Jamboree.

Answer Key: Intensive and Reflexive Pronouns

1. you. Indirect object of "sent."
2. me. Object of the preposition "by."
3. I. Subject of the verb "would be."
4. you. Subject of the verb "can come."
5. me. Object of the preposition "but."
6. me. Indirect object of "were given."
7. you. Subject of the verb "have."

Please note that not all uses of intensive and reflexive pronouns are out of bounds. The following examples are **correct**:

If you want a clean shirt tomorrow, you'll have to do the laundry yourself.

Charles was supposed to bring the caviar, but he ate it all himself in the car on the way to the party.

I surprised myself by sticking to my diet for three days before buying cupcakes.

We allow ourselves no more than two binges at the racetrack each month.

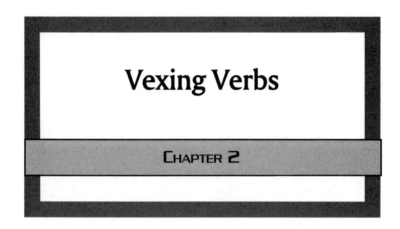

Vexing Verbs

Verbs don't always play fair. They're a huge, complicated pack of words, most of which conform to a set of rules and principles governing the different forms they take. But these rules aren't always obvious, and—wouldn't you know it—there are also lots of outliers, irregular verbs of one sort or another that require special handling and are slippery enough to cause problems for even the most careful speakers. In this chapter, we'll study three topics at the root of most of the common errors made with verbs: transitive vs. intransitive verbs, tenses of certain notorious irregular verbs, and the subjunctive mood.

Transitive and Intransitive Verbs

Here's the low-down: Transitive verbs are verbs that take a direct object in order to complete their meanings. Intransitive verbs do not take a direct object. If these terms, "transitive" and "intransitive," seem a little opaque at first, think of it this way: The transit in "transitive" refers to the idea of being conveyed across something, as in a city's transit system. Similarly, transitive verbs are those in which the action of the verb is being conveyed across from the subject to the direct object—

that is, from the person doing the acting to the person or thing on the receiving end of the action. (If the terms "subject" and "direct object" are confusing, take a little side trip back to the Grammar Review.) Take, for example, the sentence *The cat ate the canary*. Here the action of eating is being conveyed across from the subject, "cat," to the direct object, "canary." The cat was the one doing the eating, but his action of eating was worked upon, or received by, the unfortunate canary. Thus the sense of "transit" in this transitive use of the verb "ate."

Many verbs can be either transitive or intransitive depending on the way in which they're used in a sentence. But some verbs are transitive through and through. The verb "to bring" is one of these. It requires a direct object to complete its meaning, to answer the question *bring what?* You wouldn't have a meaningful sentence by saying, "he brings," but add the direct object "trouble" and you've got yourself a real sentence: *He brings trouble.*

The verb "to weep," on the other hand, can go either way. You can say, *He weeps crocodile tears*, where "tears" is the direct object—the things being wept. The presence of that direct object means that "weep" is functioning here as a transitive verb. However, you can also say, *He weeps at weddings*, and have no direct object—there's nothing on the receiving end of his action of weeping. In that case, the verb is functioning in an intransitive mode. See if you can pick out the transitive and intransitive verbs in these sentences:

Who will take the children?
(The verb here is "take." Is there something on the receiving end of the action that rounds out its meaning? Yes—the direct object is "children." So "take" is transitive.)
Who told you that?
(The verb is "told," but its meaning isn't complete—we need to know *what* was told. So the verb is transitive, and

its direct object is "that." For the record, "you" is an indirect object here.)

The train runs late every day.

(The verb "runs" is intransitive in this sentence. Although we hear something more about the way the train runs, namely that it is late every day, these words are not objects. They aren't on the receiving end of the action of running. They're describing the *manner* in which the train runs. It's possible for the verb "runs" to be used transitively as well: *She runs a restaurant downtown.* Here "restaurant" is a direct object.)

She is harboring a fugitive.

(The verb "harboring" is transitive; the direct object is "fugitive.")

The diva was unbearably self-indulgent.

(The verb "was" is a linking verb, and thus is neither transitive or intransitive: It takes a complement rather than a direct object.)

Now that you're getting the hang of this, let's look at two common errors caused by the confusing use of transitive and intransitive verbs.

9. Lie vs. Lay

Don't Say: She *lays* down for a nap after her mother visits.
Say Instead: She *lies* down for a nap after her mother visits.

Here's Why: Though "lie" and "lay" have closely related meanings, they're two entirely different verbs. "Lay" is a transitive verb, meaning to put or place or prepare something—that "something" being the verb's direct object. "Lie," on the other hand, is an intransitive verb that takes no object, and it means to be in a state of reclining. Said another way, "lying" is something you do yourself, or something an object is doing for itself—

inanimate objects such as books can be said to be in a state of reclining as well as people can. "Laying," on the other hand, is more action-oriented. It's something a person is *doing to* another thing. For example, you may lay (not lie) a book on a table, after which the book may be said to be lying (not laying) on the table. The following are correct uses of "lie" and "lay":

Lie down and go to sleep.
(Not lay down—we're not asking this person to put or place something else down, we're asking him to take a reclining position.)
Don't just lie there, do something!
(Same thing—we're talking about a person in a state of reclining.)
He lays down the law at his house.
(Here things are different—no one's reclining; in fact, this man seems busy. He's putting something down, in this case the law, which is the direct object. So the transitive verb "lays" is correct.)
She is laying the foundation for a takeover.
(Again, she's putting something in place, the foundation. This isn't about reclining.)
That dog of yours is lying on the couch again.
(Here we *are* talking about reclining, a thing the dog is happily doing for itself, so "lying" is correct.)
Just let it lie.
(The "it" here isn't having anything done to it; it's just lying there. "Lie" is the correct choice.)

Perhaps the trickiest aspect of "lie" and "lay," however, is what happens when you're describing something that happened in the past or is to happen in the future. The forms of the two verbs look more similar then, because some of the "lie" forms have an "a" in them. For example, the past tense of "lie" is "lay." Here's a chart to help you keep the verb forms straight.

	Lie	**Lay**
Present	Today I *lie* on the couch.	Today I *lay* the sod down.
Present Continuous	I *am lying* on the couch.	I *am laying* the sod down.
Future	I *will lie* on the couch tomorrow.	I *will lay* the sod down tomorrow.
Past	I *lay* on the couch yesterday.	I *laid* the sod down yesterday.
Past Perfect	I *had lain* on the couch just before he arrived.	I *had laid* the sod down just before he arrived.

Three rules can help guide you through the "lay/lie" maze:

1. "Lie" is about the state of reclining or rest, and "lay" is about putting or placing something.
2. Every form of "lay" must take an object.
3. No form of the verb "lie," meaning to recline, has a "d" in it.

Here are a few more examples of incorrect and correct uses of these two verbs:

Instead of It <u>laid</u> there for weeks, *say* It <u>lay</u> there for weeks.

(Let's look to our three rules to see why "lay" is correct here. First, the meaning—we're talking about something in a state of rest, not putting or placing something. That tells us we're in the "lie" category. Second, objects—there's no object here. More confirmation that we should be dealing with "lie" and not "lay." Third, tense forms—"laid" has to be wrong when we're dealing with the verb "lie" because it has a "d" in it, and no form of "lie" has a "d." "Lay" is the correct past tense of "lie.")

Instead of Amy had just <u>laid</u> down when he called, *say* Amy had just <u>lain</u> down when he called.

("Had lain" is correct because it's part of the "lie" family, its past perfect tense to be exact, and again, we're talking about a person doing her own reclining. And remember, once you know that you should be using "lie" instead of "lay," you know that any form with a "d" in it is out of bounds.)

Instead of By the time we leave next week, we will have <u>lain</u> some ground rules for the kids, *say* By the time we leave next week, we will have <u>laid</u> some ground rules for the kids.

(Even when things get tricky with tenses, the same rules apply. The meaning here? We're talking about putting something in place, namely the ground rules. The rules are a direct object. So we know we want the verb "lay." Then all we have to do is get the tense form right...and remembering that the forms with "d" belong to "lay," we know that "will have laid" is correct.)

10. Sit vs. Set

Don't Say: Just *set* there for a minute while I check it for you.

Say Instead: Just *sit* there for a minute while I check it for you.

Here's Why: Like "lie" and "lay," "sit" and "set" are a pair of transitive and intransitive verbs with related meanings. "Set" means to put or to place something somewhere or to put it in motion. It is always transitive, and thus always needs an object. "Sit," on the other hand, is virtually always intransitive. It means, in the case of people, to be in a seated position, or in the case of things, to be at rest. It almost never takes an object, because the sitting usually isn't being done *to* anything. The exception would be something such as *He sat them down for*

84

a talk, but that's rare. Here are some correct examples of these two verbs in action:

Please set down that priceless vase.
("Set" is transitive—its direct object is "vase.")
Why don't you sit a little closer to me?
("Sit" is intransitive—no object.)
He sat over there for hours without moving.
("Sat" is intransitive—no object.)
She set out bad cookies and weak punch.
("Set" is transitive—direct objects are "cookies" and "punch.")
I swear, I was just sitting there, minding my own business!
("Sitting" is intransitive—no object.)
He was just setting down the safe when the police caught him.
("Setting" is transitive—the direct object is "safe.")

Test: Transitive and Intransitive Verbs

Please circle the correct choice.

1. After the party he (laid, lay) on the couch and stared at the ceiling.
2. They left all the dishes (laying, lying) on the kitchen counter.
3. It took them more than two months to build the patio because they had never (lain, laid) bricks before.
4. The garden will be entirely choked by weeds if you just (lay, lie) around the house all day.
5. Every time he walks into my office he (lays, lies) his paperwork on the computer.
6. The diamonds had (lain, lay, laid) in the safe since 1973.
7. Bob hasn't read the paper since March, when he (laid, lay) his best reading glasses down somewhere and couldn't find them again.

8. I'll just (lay, lie) in the hammock all afternoon with a glass of lemonade.

9. They had just (sit, set) out all the china plates when the earthquake hit.

10. The pin was (laying, lying) on the chair when she (sat, set) down on it.

11. The cats were (sitting, setting) on the clean shirts that he had (sat, set) on the bed.

12. I'll (set, sit) here quietly until you stop shouting.

Answer Key: Transitive and Intransitive Verbs

1. lay. Past tense of "lie."

2. lying. Participle of "lie."

3. laid. Past perfect of "lay."

4. lie. Present of "lie."

5. lays. Present of "lay."

6. lain. Past perfect of "lie."

7. laid. Past tense of "lay."

8. lie. Future of "lie."

9. set. Past perfect of "set."

10. lying, sat. Past continuous of "lie"; past of "sit."

11. sitting, set. Past continuous of "sit"; past perfect of "set."

12. sit. Future of "sit."

A Lesson on Verb Tenses

Verb tenses tell us the time of the action in question. There are six tenses in all, broken into two groups: the simple tenses, and their confidently named cousins, the perfect tenses. The simple tenses are, well, simple:

❏ The **present tense** is used to show an action or a state of being that is occurring in the present or that is commonly regarded as true. Here are two examples of the present tense:

She <u>learns</u> quickly.

Children <u>watch</u> too much television.

❑   The **past tense** is used to show that something happened in the past, as in:

He <u>traveled</u> for a week.

Jenny <u>went</u> home sick yesterday.

Most verbs usually form the past tense by adding a "d" or an "ed" to the present tense form; for example, "risk" becomes "risked" and "talk" becomes "talked."

❑   The **future tense** shows that the action hasn't happened yet. It is formed by combining the future tense of the verb "to be" with the present-tense form of the main verb. "They go" becomes "they will go," "he arrives" becomes "he will arrive" and "I walk" becomes "I shall walk." (See the section up ahead on the verb "to be" for more good stuff on the whole "shall" vs. "will" dilemma.)

The perfect tenses are used to indicate that an action has been completed at the point in time to which you're referring. The three perfect tenses correspond to the three simple tenses:

❑   The **present-perfect tense** shows that at the time you're speaking, the action has been completed; for example, *I have stopped eating candy*. The present perfect is formed by combining the verb "have" or "has" with the past participle form of the main verb. "Past participle" simply means, for regular verbs, the past-tense form ending in "d" or "ed." Here are examples of the present perfect tense:

She <u>has spared</u> him.

The Smiths <u>have</u> finally <u>mowed</u> that lawn.

You <u>have dropped</u> a few pounds.

❑   The **past perfect tense** indicates that an action was completed before some specific time in the past; for example, *She had waited there for an hour when John arrived*. The past perfect is formed by combining "had" with the past participle of the main verb. More examples are:

87

They <u>had dropped</u> him from the club by then.

You had not yet <u>landed</u> that account when I joined the firm.

Although he pretended to be a novice, Tom <u>had sailed</u> this bay many times.

❏   The **future perfect tense** shows that an action will be completed at some specific point in the future. It is formed by combining "will have" or "shall have" with the past participle of the main verb. Examples are:

Before the evening ends, I <u>shall have danced</u> with Henry.

Her carriage <u>will have turned</u> into a pumpkin by midnight.

They <u>will have opened</u> all the gifts by the time the singing telegram comes.

The previous examples show that verb tenses take many forms, but you may have noticed a pattern: all these variations are built on what are known as a verb's three *principal parts*: the *present-tense form*, the *past-tense form*, and the *past participle*—the last of which is used to create the perfect tenses. If you know the principal parts of a verb, you won't have trouble forming the six tenses correctly. To illustrate, here are the principal parts of a few regular verbs:

	Present Tense *present time*	Past Tense *past time*	Past Participle *with have, had, has*
To Look	Look	Looked	Looked
To Wish	Wish	Wished	Wished
To Hunt	Hunt	Hunted	Hunted

Most of us don't have much trouble choosing the correct forms of regular verbs such as those in the previous examples. But irregular verbs are another story. Their tense forms often follow a pattern, but a less common one. And because their pattern is less common, some of these forms sound just odd enough to seem wrong even when they're right. A perfect example is the past perfect tense of the irregular verb "swim": *Stewart had swum 20 yards before the others were in the water.* "Swum?" To many of us it sounds positively wrong. But it's correct, and there are lots of similar examples. The only remedy, unfortunately, is to learn the appropriate forms the old-fashioned way—by memory. The following errors address a few of the most problematic members of this irregular group. Before we move on to them, however, we need to take an up-close and personal look at that most irregular of the irregulars, the verb "to be."

Forms of the Verb "to Be" Across the Six Tenses

"To be" is truly the king of the verbs. It's the most commonly employed verb in the language, used not only as a linking verb, but also as a helping verb, as we saw in some of the tense examples. But its forms are extremely irregular and usually bear little resemblance to the word "be." The following is a breakdown of the various forms "to be" takes in each of the six tenses as it changes to correspond in person and number with a subject. (Check the Grammar Review for a brushup on the terms "person" and "number" if you need to.)

Present Tense of "to Be"

	Singular	Plural
First Person	I *am*	We *are*
Second Person	You *are*	You *are*
Third Person	He/she/it *is*	They *are*

Past Tense of "to Be"

	Singular	Plural
First Person	I *was*	We *were*
Second Person	You *were*	You *were*
Third Person	He/she/it *was*	They *were*

Future Tense of "to Be"

	Singular	Plural
First Person	I *shall be*	We *shall be*
Second Person	You *will be*	You *will be*
Third Person	He/she/it *will be*	They *will be*

Present Perfect Tense of "to Be"

	Singular	Plural
First Person	I *have been*	We *have been*
Second Person	You *have been*	You *have been*
Third Person	He/she/it *has been*	They *have been*

Past Perfect Tense of "to Be"

	Singular	Plural
First Person	I *had been*	We *had been*
Second Person	You *had been*	You *had been*
Third Person	He/she/it *had been*	They *had been*

Future Perfect Tense of "to Be"

	Singular	Plural
First Person	I *shall have been*	We *shall have been*
Second Person	You *will have been*	You *will have been*
Third Person	He/she/it *will have been*	They *will have been*

"Shall" and "Will"

Grammar and usage experts get themselves into a lather on the finer points of this issue, and the English have an elaborate system that Americans are sometimes taught in school but stubbornly refuse to use. But we'll spare you the English system here. Just keep in mind that in formal (American) speech or writing, "shall" is the correct form of "to be" for the first person ("I" or "we") in the future and future perfect tenses. Clearly, though, "shall" is not a word you hear every day, and the negative contraction of "shall," "shan't" (the functional equivalent of "won't"), sounds downright odd to American ears. A sentence such as *I shan't have any grits today, thank you* would draw stares at your local diner. Most Americans simply use "will" and "won't" in place of "shall" and "shan't," and it would be hard to find someone who frowns on this in ordinary conversation. However, when you wish to write or speak with the highest degree of precision and formality, use "shall" in the first person. And we shan't trouble you any more on this matter.

Tricky Verb Tenses

Now let's take a look at some of the most common errors people make with verb tenses.

11. Do

> **Don't Say:** Brooks felt like a man of virtue when he had *did* the laundry.
> **Say Instead:** Brooks felt like a man of virtue when he had *done* the laundry.

Here's Why: The principal parts of the verb "to do" are "do," "did," and "done." I do, I did, I have done. So anytime you're playing with one of the perfect tenses, that is, where you're using helping verbs such as "have" or "had," you need to use the past participle, "done." Here are some more examples of the proper tense forms of "to do":

> She <u>does</u> her chores when forced to.
> She <u>did</u> her chores when forced to.
> She <u>has done</u> her chores when forced to.
> She <u>had done</u> her chores when she had been forced to.
> She <u>will have done</u> her chores only when she has been forced to.

12. Burst

> **Don't Say:** Well, Hal's bubble certainly *busted* when the truth came out.
> **Say Instead:** Well, Hal's bubble certainly *burst* when the truth came out.

Here's Why: The principal parts of "to burst" are—get this—"burst," "burst," and "burst." It bursts today, it burst yesterday, it will have burst by tomorrow. Once you remember that, it's impossible for you to choose the wrong form. "Bust" is not the past tense of "burst," but a slang variant of it, used in informal speech to mean both "burst" and "break." Most speakers don't accept "bust" as a verb in formal speech or writing, so you should avoid it. Instead of saying, *I can't come to work today because I <u>busted</u> my knee*, say, *I can't come to work today because I <u>broke</u> my knee*. And if you feel the urge to use "bust" as the past tense of "burst," resist it: "burst" has a perfectly good past tense of its own, and doesn't need any help, thank you. Here are some examples that illustrate the point:

> Lydia <u>bursts</u> through doors.
> Lydia <u>burst</u> through the door yesterday.
> Lydia <u>has burst</u> through many doors.

Some day, Lydia <u>will have burst</u> through one door too many.

13. Dive

Don't Say: Are you sure that Burt *has dove* from this high a cliff before?

Say Instead: Are you sure that Burt *has dived* from this high a cliff before?

Here's Why: The principal parts of "to dive" are "dive," "dived" or (less formally) "dove," and "dived." When using the past tense, many speakers now consider either "dove" or "dived" acceptable, although conservative speakers greatly prefer "dived"—accepted usage is slowly changing on this one. But when you're forming the perfect tenses, as we did here, with "has," you must use the past participle, and that's "dived." Here are a few more examples:

Shelly <u>dives</u> into the dullest projects.
Shelly <u>dived</u> into the dullest projects.
(Less conservative speakers will also accept "dove" in this sentence.)
Shelly <u>has dived</u> into the dullest projects.
I'm sure Shelly <u>will have dived</u> into another dull project by the time we return.

The next five errors involve verbs that share a common pattern: drink, swim, ring, sing, and spring.

14. Drink

Don't Say: Reggie, *have you drank* the best wines from your cellar yet?

Say Instead: Reggie, *have you drunk* the best wines from your cellar yet?

Here's Why: The principal parts of "to drink" are "drink," "drank," and "drunk." I drink now, I drank yesterday, I have drunk before. The verb "drink" is part of a group of irregular verbs with similar vowel changes across the tenses—an "i" in the present changing to an "a" in the past tense and a "u" for the past participle. Here are more examples featuring "drink":

Joe <u>drinks</u> a horrible protein shake in the morning.
Joe <u>drank</u> a horrible protein shake in the morning.
Joe <u>has drunk</u> a horrible protein shake every morning for years.

15. Swim

> **Don't Say:** She *had swam* 40 lengths of the pool by the time the lifeguard noticed her.
> **Say Instead:** She *had swum* 40 lengths of the pool by the time the lifeguard noticed her.

Here's Why: "Swim" follows the same pattern as "drink." Its principal parts are "swim," "swam," and "swum." I swim today, I swam yesterday, I shall have swum by tomorrow. Additional examples are:

Jack <u>swims</u> until he looks like a prune.
Jack <u>swam</u> until he looked like a prune.
Jack <u>had swum</u> until he looked like a prune, so we made him get out of the water.

16. Ring

> **Don't Say:** Surely it didn't bother Murray that I *rung* the bell 30 times?
> **Say Instead:** Surely it didn't bother Murray that I *rang* the bell 30 times?

Here's Why: Maybe you're ahead of us already—"ring" works the same way that "drink" and "swim" do. Its principal parts are "ring," "rang," and "rung." I ring, I rang, I have rung. More examples are:

> Jennifer's ears <u>ring</u> after she goes to concerts.
> Jennifer's ears <u>rang</u> after she went to the concert.
> Jennifer's ears <u>have rung</u> after she goes to concerts, so she's getting some earplugs for the next one.

17. Sing

> **Don't Say:** Martin will *have sang* in every state by next year.
> **Say Instead:** Martin will *have sung* in every state by next year.

Here's Why: Again, this one fits the pattern: the principal parts are "sing," "sang," and "sung." I sing, I sang, I had sung. Other examples are:

> Jerry <u>sings</u> bad show tunes in the shower.
> Jerry <u>sang</u> bad show tunes in the shower.
> Jerry <u>has sung</u> bad show tunes in the shower for the last time.

18. Spring

> **Don't Say:** The weeds *had* already *sprang* up by the time Doris decided which pesticide to use.
> **Say Instead:** The weeds *had* already *sprung* up by the time Doris decided which pesticide to use.

Here's Why: If you're getting a little bored with the "-ing," "-ang," "-ung" pattern, at least this one has a little twist: The principal parts are "spring," "sprang," or "sprung," and "sprung." I spring, I sprang, I shall have sprung. It's okay to use "sprung" in the past tense, as in "she sprung to life," although "sprang" seems to be a little more common. What you can't do is use "sprang" in place of "sprung" for the perfect tenses. It has to be "has, had, or have sprung." Additional examples are:

> Betty <u>springs</u> to attention whenever she sees the flag.
> Betty <u>sprang</u> *or* <u>sprung</u> to attention whenever she saw the flag.
> Betty <u>had sprung</u> to attention so many times during the parade that her knees gave out.

19. Hang

> **Don't Say:** They *hung* people for stealing chickens back then.
> **Say Instead:** They *hanged* people for stealing chickens back then.

Here's Why: The verb "to hang" is odd in that the forms vary according to whether you're using the verb in reference to an execution or in the usual sense of suspending something. Normally, "hang" follows the same pattern as "drink" and the other verbs we've just been looking at: its principal parts are "hang," "hung," and "hung." She hangs the picture, she hung it, she had hung it. But when you're talking about executions, the principal parts are "hang," "hanged," and "hanged." He'll hang at dawn, he was hanged at dawn yesterday, they have hanged him for stealing.

20. Drive

> **Don't Say:** We must *have drove* in circles for two hours before she finally asked for directions.
> **Say Instead:** We must *have driven* in circles for two hours before she finally asked for directions.

96

Here's Why: The principal parts of "to drive" are "drive," "drove," and "driven." I drive, I drove, I had driven. Most people know to use "drove" for the past tense, but they get confused about the perfect tenses, as in our example here, and use either "drove" or "drived" instead of "driven." Here are some more correct examples:

I <u>drove</u> home by myself.
I <u>had</u> not <u>driven</u> a bulldozer until yesterday.
Those kids <u>will have driven</u> me crazy by the time they leave.

21. Ought

Don't Say: We *had ought* to call first before we bring guests.
Say Instead: We *ought* to call first before we bring guests.

Here's Why: "Ought" has only one form, and that's "ought." It is a helping verb designed to work with other verbs to indicate that something should be done. No matter what tense the main verb in the sentence is in, "ought" never changes form. It never takes a helping verb such as "had" for itself. One other point worth mentioning about the verb "ought" is that it should always be followed by the infinitive form of a verb, that is, the form with the word "to" in front of it, as in *We <u>ought to come</u> at Christmas, you <u>ought to slow</u> down, they <u>ought not to take</u> the test next week.*

Finally, to complete our look at verb forms, there are two errors that call for the verb form of the infinitive.

22. Be sure and

Don't Say: *Be sure and* try the sea urchin omelette.
Say Instead: *Be sure to* try the sea urchin omelette.

Here's Why: The phrase "be sure" should be followed by either the infinitive form of a verb—"to try," in our example— or by a complete clause *be sure <u>that you</u> try the sea urchin omelette.*

23. Try and

Don't Say: *Try and* be home before your curfew this time.
Say Instead: *Try to* be home before your curfew this time.

Here's Why: Same thing as in the previous example: You can't use "and" where an infinitive form of the verb is required.

Test: Tricky Verb Tenses

Please circle the correct choice.

1. They (did, done) everything they could to make him uncomfortable.
2. She (had did, had done) nothing to prepare for her in-laws' visit.
3. The whole house was flooded after the pipes (busted, burst).
4. The thief ran to the window and (dived, dove) through it head-first.
5. Like most people, Horace had never (dived, dove) into a vat of Jell-O before.
6. After slathering her burrito with Tabasco sauce, she (drank, drunk) all the water she could find.
7. We had (drank, drunk) so much coffee that we were up until 4 in the morning.
8. Peter (swam, swum) out to the island and stayed there all afternoon.
9. Barbara claims that she has often (swam, swum) 40 laps before breakfast.
10. The phone had (rang, rung) eight times before he got up to answer it.

11. They (rang, rung) the doorbell, (dove, dived) into the bushes, and (lay, laid) there, giggling.

12. Cindy divorced him because he (sprang, sprung) out of bed every morning at 5 and (sang, sung) loudly as he dressed.

13. The tiger had (sprang, sprung) before we even realized he was there.

14. Bill had (sang, sung) three verses before realizing that the rest of the choir was singing something else.

15. She (hang, hung, hanged) the keys on a hook by the door.

16. They (hung, hanged) the bandits from the old cottonwood tree.

17. We have (hung, hanged) all the plants from the ceiling so the cats can't eat them.

18. The sheriff will have (hung, hanged) Quick-draw Mahoney before you can get there with the governor's pardon.

19. I had (drove, driven, drived) for hours before realizing I was on the wrong road.

20. His endless stream of knock-knock jokes (drove, driven, drived) me to distraction.

21. Cecily (had ought, ought) to ask nicely before she borrows your car.

22. (Be sure and, Be sure to) wear your raincoat if you have front row seats at the mud wrestling championship.

23. (Try and, Try to) be nice to your mother-in-law.

Answer Key: Tricky Verb Tenses

1. did. Past of "do."
2. had done. Past perfect of "do."
3. burst. Past of "burst."
4. dived. Older form, and still preferred by conservative speakers; some speakers increasingly also find "dove" acceptable for the simple past tense.

5. dived. Past perfect of "dived."
6. drank. Past of "drink."
7. drunk. Past perfect of "drink."
8. swam. Past of "swim."
9. swum. Past perfect of "swim."
10. rung. Past perfect of "rang."
11. rang, dived (preferred) *or* dove, lay. All are past tense.
12. sprang, sang. Both are past tense.
13. sprung. Past perfect of "spring."
14. sung. Past perfect of "sing."
15. hung. Past of "hang."
16. hanged. Past of "hang," correct form for execution.
17. hung. Present perfect of "hang."
18. hanged. Present perfect of "hang," special form for execution.
19. driven. Past perfect of "drive."
20. drove. Past of "drive."
21. ought. Ought has only on form: "ought."
22. Be sure to. "Be sure" should be followed by an infinitive.
23. Try to. "Try" should be followed by an infinitive.

The Subjunctive Mood

As noted in the Grammar Review, the subjunctive mood is used to indicate a hypothetical situation, a wish, or a circumstance contrary to fact. Examples of the last might be, "If I were rich," said by someone who is not, or "If I were you," because one could never actually *be* the other person. The subjunctive is also used occasionally to make a suggestion or a demand. Here are some uses of the subjunctive:

❑ **Hypothetical Situation:** If we were to leave on Friday, we'd get there early.

- ❑ **Wish:** I wish I <u>were</u> on the morning shift.
- ❑ **Contrary to Fact:** If I <u>were</u> you, I would run for office.
- ❑ **Suggestion:** I suggest she <u>take</u> her things with her on the trip.
- ❑ **Demand:** His teacher demanded that Ed <u>show</u> up on time.

You'll notice that in most of these examples, the form of the verb doesn't seem to match the person and number of the subject—it says, "I were" instead of "I am," "she take" instead of "she takes" and "Ed show" instead of "Ed shows." There is a whole thicket full of odd-sounding constructions in the subjunctive mood, most of them used only in poetic or parliamentary contexts. However, all you really need to know in order to navigate the subjunctive waters successfully for most occasions are two rules. Here's the less important one first:

In the subjunctive mood, verbs in the present tense drop the "s" they normally end with in the third person. In other words, instead of *I suggest she <u>attends</u>*, it should be *I suggest she <u>attend</u>*.

The most significant rule, though, is for the verb "to be," because that's the verb most commonly used in the subjunctive mood today. And the rule is this:

The past tense form "was" is always replaced by "were" in the subjunctive mood, no matter what the person and number of the subject is. For example, you shouldn't say *If he <u>was</u> there, this wouldn't have happened.* You should say *If he <u>were</u> there, this wouldn't have happened.*

How can you be sure you're dealing with the subjunctive so you know whether "were" is correct? Here's a litmus test: First, check for key words, such as "if," "as though," and "wish."

They are used in all the moods but are so common in the subjunctive that their presence in a sentence increases the odds that that's the mood you're dealing with. Second, ask yourself if the sentence is about an uncertainty, a wish, a suggestion, a demand, or a condition clearly contrary to fact, such as *If wishes were horses then beggars would ride*. If it is, you're definitely in the subjunctive and you need to change your "wases" to "weres."

24. If I Was vs. If I Were

Don't Say: If I *was* you, I wouldn't wear horizontal stripes.
Say Instead: If I *were* you, I wouldn't wear horizontal stripes.

Here's Why: We need "were" instead of "was" here because we're in the subjunctive mood. We know it's the subjunctive because the signs are there: the use of "if," and the condition contrary to fact—in this case, the fact that I cannot be you. Let's look at a few more examples of the correct use of "was" and "were":

I wish Jane <u>were</u> planning to go with us.
(The expression of a wish is the key indicator that we're in the subjunctive mood here, and that makes this use of "were" correct.)
If Tom <u>were</u> in charge instead of Maria, we'd be fine!
(The meaning here is that Tom is not in charge, so the condition referred to is in opposition with reality. Therefore, we're in the subjunctive and "were" is correct.)
If Jack <u>was</u> at home, Sue must have been with him.
(Despite the "if" that begins this sentence, we're not in the subjunctive in this case. The meaning of the sentence is not a condition contrary to fact, or a wish or a suggestion. The implication is that Jack probably was at home. So "was" is correct.)

Test: The Subjunctive

Please circle the correct choice.

1. I wish I (was, were) anywhere else but here with you.

2. If he (was, were) a little taller, they'd be a really cute couple.

3. Her boss demanded that she (spend, spends) two weeks learning to use the new software.

4. If you (are, were) a color, what color would you be?

5. You would have to turn right at this intersection if you (are, were) going to church, but since you (are, were) going to the racetrack instead, turn left.

6. She wished she (was, were) (lying, laying) on a beach rather than (sitting, setting) at her desk.

7. I wouldn't get too close to that bear if I (was, were) you.

8. If the key (was, were) there this morning, then it couldn't have just walked away.

9. The doctor suggested that he (eat, eats) more vegetables and less butter.

10. Fred and Bob are on their way. If Fred (is, were) driving his sports car, they'll get here early, but if Bob (is, were) driving his golf cart, they won't be in time for dinner.

Answer Key: The Subjunctive

1. were. Subjunctive; wish.

2. were. Subjunctive; condition contrary to fact.

3. spend. Subjunctive; demand.

4. were. Subjunctive; condition contrary to fact.

5. were, are. The first verb describes a condition contrary to fact, and thus requires the subjunctive; the second verb describes what's actually going on, and thus requires the indicative.

6. were, lying, sitting. Subjunctive; condition contrary to fact. Participles of lie and sit.

103

7. were. Subjunctive; condition contrary to fact.

8. was. Indicative; the assumption here is that the key actually was there.

9. eat. Subjunctive; suggestion.

10. is, is. Indicative; the speaker is not describing conditions contrary to fact, but two alternative possibilities.

Ambiguous Agreements

CHAPTER 3

One of the most common mistakes people make when they're putting together a sentence is to choose forms of words that don't agree with each other. When we say "agree" here, we mean that the words have to correspond in both *person and number*. "Agreeing in person" means that a first-person noun such as "I" needs a first-person verb such as "am" to make its life complete (rather than a third-person verb like "are"). "Agreeing in number" means that a singular subject such as "lobster" would like nothing better than to settle down with a singular verb such as "is" (rather than a plural verb such as "are").

Most sentences present few problems with agreement; we don't have to think about it much. If you grew up speaking English, for example, it probably never would occur to you to say, *I are sure that lobster are poisonous*. Instead, you'd say, *I am sure that lobster is poisonous*, and your grammar would be correct, even if your concern about the lobster was not.

People run into trouble with agreement only when their sentences start to get complicated. By far the most common error happens when a sentence's subject is modified by so many little phrases that you forget what the subject is—which brings us to our first agreement error: subjects with complex modifiers.

25. Subjects With Complex Modifiers

Don't Say: Gloria realized that the functions of Ralph's expensive new computer *was* about to be explained to her in detail.

Say Instead: Gloria realized that the functions of Ralph's expensive new computer *were* about to be explained to her in detail.

Here's Why: The subject of the verb "were" is "functions," and because "functions" is plural, it needs a plural verb: *functions were*. The sentence only gets confusing because of the phrase "of Ralph's expensive new computer." That phrase is parked right next to the verb, doing its best to look like a subject. But it's not; it's a mere modifier. Its sole purpose is to tell us something about the verb's real subject, "functions." When you're trying to make a sentence's subject and verb agree, then, the first thing you have to do is make sure you've got the real subject, not a measly little modifier trying to put on airs.

Here are some more correct examples of verbs that agree with subjects rather than their modifiers:

The people with the cute racing stripe on their truck were driving in the center of the road.
("Were" agrees with "people," not "stripe" or "truck.")
The telephone with all the fancy buttons and lights was far too complicated for me to use.
("Was" agrees with "telephone," not "buttons and lights.")

We'll be seeing a lot more of this kind of error later on, particularly in the tests for this chapter. Complex modifiers can be a complicating factor in the other two kinds of errors that give people the most trouble in this area: agreement between compound subjects and verbs, and agreement with indefinite pronouns. Let's take them one at a time.

Agreement With Compound Subjects

Even if a subject doesn't come breezing into the sentence with a string of modifiers trailing after it, it can still give us agreement headaches if it's what we call a *compound subject*—if it has more than one part. Do you say, *Jack and he is going to the game*, or, *Jack and he are going*? And if you're not sure which of them will attend, do you say, *Either Jack or he is going* or *Either Jack or he are going*? Here are two rules to guide you:

First, the rule on subjects joined by "and":

With one exception, all subjects joined together by the word "and" are considered plural, because they refer to more than one person or thing. So you'll need to use a plural verb in order to have agreement.

In the previous example, the correct form would be *Jack and he are going to the game*. The exception is when the parts joined by "and" are meant to refer to the same person or thing, or to something commonly considered to be a unit. Two examples are *cereal and milk is a typical choice for breakfast* and *Her longtime nurse and companion* (meaning that these are the same person) *is coming to tea*.

Now for compound subjects joined by "or" or "nor." Unlike subjects joined by "and," the very role of "or" and "nor" is to separate, to tell us that it's not *both* things, but one thing or the other that the verb applies to. So the rule is:

Subjects joined by "or" or "nor" are not considered as a group, and the verb's person and number should agree with those of the subject's individual parts.

There are three possible scenarios here. If both parts are singular, as in the subject *Mary or Donna*, then the verb is

107

singular. If they're both plural, as in the subject *Neither the girls nor the boys*, the verb is plural. And in really tricky sentences where you have one of each, such as *Either Tony or his daughters*, the verb should agree with whatever part of the subject it's closest to in the sentence; for example, *either Tony or his daughters are* but *either the daughters or their father is*. Let's look at a few examples of common errors in agreement between compound subjects and their verbs.

26. Subjects Joined by "And"

> **Don't Say:** One and one *is* two.
> **Say Instead:** One and one *are* two.

Here's Why: The singular verb, "is," is wrong here, because it doesn't agree with the compound subject, "one and one," which is plural. Remember the rule: When you're referring to two or more people or things together as your subject, the verb must be plural to match.

Tip: Here's an easy tip for remembering the "and" rule: Ask yourself if you can substitute the plural pronouns "we," "they," or "you" without changing the basic meaning of the sentence. If you can, then your verb should be plural, too. Similar correct examples are:

Harry and I <u>are</u> her favorites.
He and I <u>are</u> at work by 8.
(In this case, instead of "he and I," you could have substituted "we." That's the signal that the verb should be plural—you'd never say "We <u>am</u> at work by 8.")
The director and her assistant <u>speak</u> at every production meeting.
She and Susan and Bill <u>are</u> going to the movie.

Tip: Try using the substitution tip here. Instead of "She and Susan and Bill," you could have said "They." And you'd never say "they is," only "they are." So the plural "are" is what you need. Similar correct examples are:

> My attorney and my accountant and my husband and I are invited to the meeting.
> The father and the mother and their daughter always try to do what's right.
> The lumber and the bricks and the cement have been delivered.

27. "Either/Or" and "Neither/Nor"

Don't Say: Either Tom or Henry *have* lost the book.
Say Instead: Either Tom or Henry *has* lost the book.

Here's Why: Remember that "or" and "nor" separate the two parts of the subject. The idea is that it's one or the other of these guys, not both together, who has lost the book. And because each of these subjects, Tom and Henry, is singular, the plural verb "have" is incorrect.

Tip: Ask yourself: Would I say, *Henry have lost it* or *Tom have lost it*? No, You'd pick "has." Related correct examples are:

> Either an apple or a banana is in his lunch bag every day.
> (Both parts of the subject are singular, the verb is singular too.)
> Either Carrie or Maria has been baby-sitting for them.
> (Singular subjects, singular verb.)
> Either the O'Malley's or the Smiths have the best garden each year.
> (Plural subjects, plural verb.)
> Either Diane or her parents are going to pay the bill.
> (One singular and one plural subject. Verb is plural because it's next to the plural half of the subject.)

109

Either the two cats or the dog is going to have to go. (One singular, one plural subject. Singular verb next to singular subject.)

> **Don't Say:** Neither the horse nor the trainer *were* ready.
> **Say Instead:** Neither the horse nor the trainer *was* ready.

Here's Why: Same thing as with "either/or": The "nor" divides the two parts of the subject and we consider them separately. Each part—in this case, "horse" and "trainer"—is a singular subject, so the plural verb, "were," is incorrect.

Tip: Would you say, *the horse were ready* or *the trainer were ready*? No. That's the signal that you need the singular form "was." Related correct examples are:

Neither the brushes nor the paints were on the table.
Neither Dave nor Leslie is going to the conference.
Neither the couch nor the chairs are being used.

28. Subjects Joined by "Or"

> **Don't Say:** Her parents or society *are* to blame.
> **Say Instead:** Her parents or society *is* to blame.

Here's Why: Again, the same rule applies whether we have "either/or" or just plain "or." The two parts of the subject are considered separately. In this case, "parents" is plural and "society" is singular. Remember, when you have one singular and one plural in your subject, the verb should agree with whichever part it's closest to. But here we have the plural verb "are" right after society, which is singular, so that's incorrect.

Tip: Would you say *society are to blame*? No, you'd say *society is to blame*, so you need "is" here. Similarly:

Leo or Nora has to pick up Jan before 9.
Bees or wasps were swarming nearby.

The camera or the lights <u>are</u> scheduled for replacement next month.

Test: Compound Subjects and Verbs

Please circle the correct choice.

1. Each morning, Rachel and Joanna (runs, run) past my window on their way to the train station.

2. The kids next door and the dog (has, have) been trampling all over our flowers.

3. Either the kids next door or the dog (has, have) been trampling all over our flowers.

4. Either the dog or the kids next door (has, have) set off the alarm we left in the flower bed.

5. Neither the computer nor Sylvia (is, are) working this morning.

6. Neither the adults nor the children (was, were) patient enough to sit through the entire movie.

7. Egbert and the man with the glass eye (was, were) talking quietly in a smoke-filled room.

8. Bob, who recently quit smoking, and I (am, are) going to the store to buy as much gum as we can carry.

9. The woman whose shoes are adorned with artificial cherries and bananas (are, is) getting all the attention.

10. All the paper clips in the office have been twisted into little animal shapes; either Frank or Larry (is, are) playing with them.

11. Either the flowers or the cats (is, are) making Gia sneeze.

12. Every week either my mother or my therapist (tell, tells) me to stop dressing as a giant hot dog.

13. Either the appetizers or the salads (contain, contains) the tainted mayonnaise.

14. We've been told by our informants that the police chief's car or mailbox (has, have) been rigged to play "Happy Birthday" when he walks by.

111

15. Something in the apartment upstairs keeps making noise; either the door or one of the windows (is, are) squeaking.

16. Neither the maniacal laughter from the basement nor the spider dangling over our heads (has, have) frightened the trick-or-treaters this year.

17. Her wicked uncle or his evil minions (has, have) hidden the key to the dungeon.

18. Every morning at 5, the chickens or the prize rooster with the purple feathers (start, starts) squawking.

Answer Key: Compound Subjects and Verbs

1. run. Compound subject with "and."

2. have. Compound subject with "and."

3. has. Either/or; closest subject ("dog") is singular.

4. have. Either/or; closest subject ("kids") is plural.

5. is. Neither/nor; closest subject ("Sylvia") is singular.

6. were. Neither/nor; closest subject ("children") is plural.

7. were. Compound subject with "and."

8. are. Compound subject with "and."

9. is. The subject ("woman") is singular; everything between "woman" and "is" only describes the subject. No matter how many things the woman has on her shoes, she's still getting all the attention.

10. is. Either/or; closest subject ("Larry") is singular.

11. are. Either/or; closest subject ("cats") is plural.

12. tells. Either/or; closest subject ("therapist") is singular.

13. contain. Either/or; the closest subject ("salads") is plural.

14. has. Either/or; the closest subject ("mailbox") is singular.

15. is. Either/or; the closest subject ("one") is singular; "of the windows" modifies "one" and can't influence the verb form.

16. has. Neither/nor; the closest subject ("spider") is singular; "dangling over our heads modifies "spider," and can't influence the verb form.

17. have. Or; closest subject ("minions") is plural.

18. starts. Or; closest subject ("rooster") is singular; "with the purple feathers" modifies "rooster," and can't influence the verb form.

Agreement With Indefinite Pronouns

Indefinite pronouns, such as "each," "everyone," and "anybody," really trip people up when it comes to agreement. They *feel* plural, as though they're referring to a whole group, so we tend to attach plural verbs to them, and we often use other plural pronouns if we need to refer back to them in the sentence. We say things such as *Each of them are to blame* and *Everyone has their coat on*, but these are errors. Fortunately, the rule is pretty simple:

> The following indefinite pronouns are always singular: one, no one, anyone, everyone, someone, anybody, somebody, nobody, everybody, each, either, and neither. So the verbs and pronouns they need to agree within a sentence have to be singular too.

Think of these words as referring not to the many individuals composing the group, but to each one member. The ultimate focus is on the one, not on the group that one may be a part of. Let's look at some common agreement errors that occur when using indefinite pronouns:

29. Each...Are

> **Don't Say:** Each of the girls *are* going to be tested.
> **Say Instead:** Each of the girls *is* going to be tested.

113

Here's Why: In the first sentence, we broke the simple rule: "Each," meaning "each one," is singular, so the plural verb "are" is wrong. Some related examples using other singular indefinite pronouns:

Instead of Either of these books <u>are</u> good, *say* Either of these books <u>is</u> good.

Instead of Only one of the teachers <u>have</u> been through the training program, *say* Only one of the teachers <u>has</u> been through the training program.

Instead of Neither of them <u>have</u> the right to go, *say*, Neither of them <u>has</u> the right to go.

30. None...Is/Are

Don't Say: He wants a jukebox, but none *are* available.
Say Instead: He wants a jukebox, but none *is* available.

Here's Why: The rules on this one are genuinely in flux. Unlike the indefinite pronouns listed earlier, "none," along with "some," "any," and "all," isn't always singular. It can be either singular or plural depending on the meaning of your sentence. The rule of thumb is: If it refers to a group in total, or to a thing as a whole, then "none" is usually viewed as singular and takes a singular verb. If it refers to a number of things, meaning your emphasis is on the quantity of the parts and not on the whole, then "none" is considered plural. In our example, *He wants a jukebox, but none are available*, we're talking about *not one* jukebox, so the plural verb, "are," is incorrect. Let's look at a few more examples:

None of the cakes <u>are</u> ready.

(Here "none" refers to a number of cakes, so the plural form "are" is correct.)

None of the cement is left.

(In this case, we're not talking about a number, we're talking about a mass of cement taken as a whole, so it's singular, and the singular verb "is" is correct.)

None of the rules were broken.

(Here we're referring to more than one rule, so the plural verb "were" is fine.)

This particular rule is pretty tough, because sometimes it's hard to tell from the context whether the meaning is plural or singular. "None" is especially tricky in this regard. Most grammarians are genuinely fuzzy about this one. Conservative speakers insist that it should always be singular. In older English it was always singular; now it is more frequently plural unless we're talking about an indefinable mass of something, such as cement or plastic or spaghetti. Very conservative speakers might also use the singular in the following sentence:

None of the students has finished the test yet.

The argument here is that the speaker means to take the students together as a single group. But it's hard for most speakers to use the singular in a sentence such as this one:

None of my brothers are going to the dance.

Again, the brothers *could* be taken together as a single group that needs a singular verb. But to most people, this sentence communicates an idea of a number of nondancing brothers. If you really want to use a singular verb, you could say something such as *Not one of my brothers is going to the dance.* So, as a rule of thumb, you're probably going to want to use a plural verb with "none." But if you feel the real meaning of the subject is singular, go with that instinct—the rule is loose enough to accommodate you.

Test: Indefinite Pronouns and Verbs

Please circle the correct choice.

1. Each of the songs (was, were) worse than the last.

2. We've asked everyone we could find, but no one (know, knows) where our pet tarantula is hiding.

3. Everyone who has seen Bill and Gloria (think, thinks) they'd look less silly if they stopped wearing each other's clothes to work.

4. Neither of them (is, are) willing to admit that other things are more important than baseball.

5. One of the movers (realize, realizes) the piano is about to fall directly on their heads.

6. I've been packed up for hours, but none of my brothers (is, are) ready to leave yet.

7. None of the paper (is, are) really suitable for engraved invitations.

8. My grandmother says that anyone who doesn't like floral wallpaper patterns (is, are) too picky for words.

9. Nobody on any of the teams (see, sees) why we should adopt the infield fly rule in mid-season.

10. Both Bob and Dave (love, loves) driving, but if either of them (drive, drives) you to the airport, I'll be extremely surprised.

11. Someone with some pretty strange ideas (has, have) sent Margaret a life-size replica of her Great Dane made entirely out of gum wrappers.

12. Anybody who (spill, spills) grape juice on my nice white carpet will have to clean it off immediately.

13. Everybody I've met for the past two days (has, have) asked me for money.

14. Whoever is putting away our spoons (is, are) making an awful racket.

15. Some of the ice in the cooler always (come, comes) in handy for treating sports injuries.

16. Some of the ice cubes (contain, contains) unusual specimens of pond life that you might not want in your drink.

17. All of us (is, are) sailing to Hawaii on a condemned barge.

18. All of the Jell-O (is, are) sliding off the tray and onto Aunt Agatha's hair.

19. (Have, has) any of the guides ever ventured so far into the jungle before?

20. Any of the plastic left over when we've finished (is, are) going to be recycled.

Answer Key: Indefinite Pronouns and Verbs

1. was. "Each" is the singular subject; "of the songs" only modifies the subject and thus cannot influence the verb form.

2. knows. "No one" is the singular subject.

3. thinks. "Everyone" is the singular subject; "who has seen Bill and Gloria" modifies "everyone."

4. is. "Neither" is the singular subject; "of them" modifies "neither."

5. realizes. "One" is the singular subject; "of the movers" modifies "one."

6. are. "None" is the subject, and takes a singular or plural verb depending on the meaning of the sentence; "brothers" refers to a quantifiable number of people who aren't ready, and thus the sentence requires a plural verb.

7. is. "Paper" refers to a group of things in total, and thus requires a singular verb.

8. is. "Anyone" is the singular subject; "who doesn't like floral wallpaper patterns" modifies "anyone."

9. sees. "Nobody" is the singular subject; "on any of the teams" modifies the subject.

117

10. love, drives. Compound subject with "and" calls for a plural verb; "either" calls for a singular verb.

11. has. "Someone" is the singular subject; "with some pretty strange ideas" modifies "someone."

12. spills. "Who" is the subject of "spills"; "who" is singular because it refers to "anybody," which is singular.

13. has. "Everybody" is the singular subject; "I've met for the past two days" is a clause modifying "everybody."

14. is. "Whoever" is the singular subject; "putting away our spoons" modifies "whoever."

15. comes. "Some" takes a singular or plural verb depending on the meaning of the sentence; here "ice" refers to a thing as a whole, and so needs a singular verb.

16. contain. Here "ice cubes" refers to a number of distinct, quantifiable things, and so "some" takes a plural verb.

17. are. "All" takes a singular or plural verb depending on the meaning of the sentence; here "us" refers to a quantifiable number of people, so the verb should be plural.

18. is. "Jell-O" refers to a thing taken as a whole, and thus takes a singular verb.

19. have. "Any," the subject of the sentence, is singular or plural depending on the meaning of the sentence; here "guides" refers to a quantifiable number of people, and thus requires a plural verb.

20. is. "Plastic" refers to a thing as a whole, so "any," the subject of the sentence, is singular and takes a singular verb.

Indefinite Pronouns and Personal Pronouns

31. Everyone...Their

Don't Say: Everyone collects *their* paycheck on Friday.
Say Instead: Everyone collects *his*—or *her*—paycheck on Friday.

Here's Why: In this case, the agreement problem isn't the verb. It's the pronoun "their" that's wrong. "Their" is plural, but what the sentence really needs is a singular pronoun to refer back to the singular subject, "everyone." Your correct pronoun choices in cases like these are "his," "her," and "it." Years ago, using "his" was the standard, regardless of whether the reference was to men or women, and the corrected version of this sentence would have been *Everyone collects his paycheck on Friday*. These days, that sort of construction is usually viewed as inappropriate, unless everyone referred to actually is male. Instead, we have a few choices. Let's look at a few ways this sentence could be corrected. Instead of *Everyone collects their paycheck on Friday*, you could say:

> Everyone collects his or her paycheck on Friday.
> Everyone collects his paycheck on Friday. (This assumes all the paycheck collectors are men.)
> Everyone collects her paycheck on Friday. (This assumes all the paycheck collectors are women.)

A note on using "his or her": It may be egalitarian, but it can also get cumbersome. Often the best thing to do is to reconfigure the sentence to sidestep the issue altogether. For example, you might say:

> Everyone collects a paycheck on Friday.
> The employees collect their paychecks on Friday.

In order to cement this down, let's look at some more examples of nonagreement and agreement between indefinite pronouns and other pronouns in a sentence:

> *Instead of* Every student was told to go to their advisor, *say* Every student was told to go to his or her advisor, *or* The students were told to go to their advisors.
> *Instead of* Anyone can get in by showing their company ID at the door, *say* Anyone can get in by showing his or her company ID at the door, *or* Employees

119

can get in by showing their company ID at the door. *Instead of* Each of the girls was showing how they swam, *say* Each of the girls was showing how she swam.

Do the "wrong" versions of these sentences still sound right to you? Don't worry. Many people use constructions such as "everyone...their." The language may be changing in this area, and it wouldn't be the first time. English once had both singular and plural forms of the second person pronoun: to address two or more people, "you" and "your" were used, but to address only one person, "thou" and "thine" were used. If we still used the singular form in English, we'd get to say a lot of sentences like this: *Thou shouldst get thy brakes serviced soon or thou wilt crash thy car into a tree.* "Thou" and "thy" gradually dropped out of the language when speakers started to use the plural "you"—a sign of how the language changes.

Today, something similar may be happening with constructions such as "everyone...their." But for now, "everyone...their" is **not considered correct** in formal speech or in writing, so you should be aware of alternatives that don't break the rules.

Test: Indefinite Pronouns and Personal Pronouns

In each of the following sentences, a **plural** pronoun such as "they" or "their" is used **incorrectly** with a **singular** indefinite pronoun such as "somebody," "everybody," "anybody," "each," "every," or "everyone." Can you suggest rewrites for each sentence? Just to make things difficult, assume that the indefinite pronouns refer to groups composed of both men and women. There are several ways to rewrite each one; we suggest multiple possibilities in the Answer Key.

1. Everyone wipes their dirty boots before they enter a fancy restaurant, so why not do the same at home?

2. As soon as the race began, each of the balloonists tried to lighten their load by tossing their picnic baskets overboard.

3. Each guest was served a fine meal and given a little bag to take home to their dog.

4. Anyone can show they care by sending flowers, but Bob and Gloria send money.

5. No one leaves before they sign the guest book and comfort the now poverty-stricken parents of the bride.

6. Nobody with any sense would leave their diamond nose ring sitting right out where anyone could slip it in their pocket.

Answer Key:
Indefinite Pronouns and Personal Pronouns

1. Everyone wipes <u>his or her</u> dirty boots before <u>he or she</u> enters a fancy restaurant, so why not do the same at home?
Or: Everyone wipes <u>his or her</u> dirty boots before entering the fancy restaurant, so why not do the same at home?
Or: <u>Guests at a fancy restaurant</u> wipe <u>their</u> dirty boots before <u>they</u> come in, so why not do the same at home?

2. As soon as the race began, each of the balloonists tried to lighten <u>his or her</u> load by tossing the picnic baskets overboard.
Or: As soon as the race began, <u>the balloonists</u> tried to lighten <u>their</u> load by tossing their picnic baskets overboard.

3. Each guest was served a fine meal and given a little bag to take home to <u>his or her</u> dog.
Or: Each guest was served a fine meal and given a little bag to take home to <u>the</u> dog.
Or: <u>The guests</u> were served a fine meal and given a little bag to take home to <u>their</u> dogs.

4. Anyone can show <u>he or she</u> cares by sending flowers, but Bob and Gloria send money.
Or: Anyone can send flowers, but Bob and Gloria send money to show <u>they</u> care.

121

Or: <u>Unimaginative people</u> send flowers to show they care, but Bob and Gloria send money.

5. No one leaves before <u>he or she</u> signs the guest book and comforts the now poverty-stricken parents of the bride. *Or:* No one may leave before <u>signing</u> the guest book and comforting the now poverty-stricken parents of the bride.

6. Nobody with any sense would leave <u>his or her</u> diamond nose ring sitting right out where anyone could slip it in his or her pocket.
Or: Nobody with any sense would leave <u>a</u> diamond nose ring sitting right out where anyone could <u>make off with it</u>.

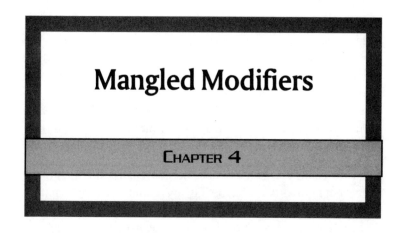

Mangled Modifiers

CHAPTER 4

"Modifiers" are a neat class of words. They're the adjectives and adverbs we use to dress up other words with color and dimension and thousands of other descriptions. And for the most part, we do a pretty good job of using them correctly. But there are a few landmines in this happy field of modifiers, and this chapter will teach you to step gracefully around them.

Adjectives vs. Adverbs

The first place people run into trouble is in distinguishing between the adjective and adverb forms of a given modifier. In these cases, the adjective is typically misapplied as an adverb.

32. Bad vs. Badly

> **Don't Say:** How can you leave me when I need you so *bad*?
> **Say Instead:** How can you leave me when I need you so *badly*?

Here's Why: "Bad" is an adjective in most cases, which means it should be used only to modify nouns and pronouns.

"Badly" is an adverb, which means it's used to modify verbs, adjectives, and other adverbs—not nouns or pronouns. In the first version of the example sentence, "bad" is being used incorrectly. It's incorrect because we are trying to modify the verb "need" to describe to what extent the need is felt; and the minute we start modifying a verb, we need to apply the adverb form, not the adjective. Here are a few more correct examples:

> I felt <u>bad</u> that you couldn't be with us.
> (Why don't we use "badly" here? Because the intention is not to modify the verb "felt" by communicating that the feeling was being done without skill. The meaning is that the feeling the person had was negative as opposed to positive. "Bad" is modifying the pronoun "I."
> Was Lou hurt <u>badly</u> when the parrot bit him?
> (Here we're describing the extent to which Lou was hurt—we're modifying the verb, so the adverb form "badly" is correct.)
> Sam wants so <u>badly</u> to go to the awards dinner.
> The stew tasted <u>bad</u>, so we fed it to the dog.

33. Real vs. Really

> **Don't Say:** Don't worry, honey, your brother will be *real* happy to take you to the prom.
> **Say Instead:** Don't worry, honey, your brother will be *really* happy to take you to the prom.

Here's Why: This error is similar to "bad" and "badly." "Real" is an adjective meaning genuine or essential. "Really" is an adverb of degree or emphasis, used in informal speech to mean very or truly. Here, where the meaning is that the brother would be very happy about escorting his sister, "really" is the appropriate choice. More examples:

Poor thing, does she believe it's a <u>real</u> diamond?

124

Mrs. Stone is going to be <u>really</u> late for her poker game.
I'm sure your concern is <u>real</u>, Susie, but we can't keep that horse in our garage.
I have to go; my mother-in-law will be here <u>really</u> soon.

34. Near vs. Nearly

Don't Say: Why, that child's *near* 6 feet tall!
Say Instead: Why, that child's *nearly* 6 feet tall!

Here's Why: Again, we're dealing with adjective vs. adverb forms. "Near" is an adjective meaning "adjacent," or "close to." The adverb "nearly" expresses degree; it means "almost." In this sentence, of course, we mean that the child is almost 6 feet tall, and that makes "nearly" the right choice. Additional correct examples:

He really struggled <u>near</u> the end of the marathon.
Joan has <u>nearly</u> finished her thesis on the social habits of gnats in the 19th century.
The model wasn't <u>nearly</u> as pretty as the woman taking her picture.
Lester was <u>near</u> enough and dumb enough to poke the gorilla with a stick.

Another common mistake made with modifiers is blurring the line between the uses of good and well, as illustrated in the following error.

35. Good vs. Well

Don't Say: I'm doing *good*; thanks for asking.
Say Instead: I'm doing *well*; thanks for asking.

Here's Why: "Good" is generally used as an adjective meaning commendable, worthy, virtuous, pleasing, or valid. "Well" is used as either an adjective describing good health—

that is, being well as opposed to sick—or as an adverb meaning to do something in a satisfactory way (he did it well); skillfully (he dances well); in a kind way (he treated her well); or to a considerable extent (he is well on his way). In this sentence (a response to the common question, "How are you doing?") the meaning is not that the speaker is off doing good deeds, it is that he is doing fine, that he is doing a satisfactory job with his day or his life. So the response, "I'm doing well," is correct. Here are more correct examples:

> Are you feeling <u>well</u>?
> You look <u>good</u> even in that ugly suit.
> She spells <u>well</u> for someone who just learned English.
> That job is working out very <u>well</u> for Joe.
> It's <u>good</u> to plan ahead, but your vacation isn't for eight more months.

Test: Adjectives vs. Adverbs

Please circle the correct choice.

1. I never thought she would date anyone who smelled so (bad, badly).
2. The cellist played so (bad, badly) that the concert was stopped by the police.
3. We should get together for root beer and crab cakes (real, really) soon.
4. Shelley assured us that the trim on her bikini was made of (real, really) fur.
5. It's a big fish all right, but the one that got away was (near, nearly) 10 feet long and as mean as a taxpayer on April 15.
6. Umberto looks (real, really) (good, well) in his flamenco costume, but he can't dance very (good, well).
7. Fred promised to be (good, well) while she was out visiting her sick grandmother, but he kept his promise (bad, badly).

Answer Key: Adjectives vs. Adverbs

1. bad.
2. badly.
3. really.
4. real.
5. nearly.
6. really, good, well.
7. good, badly.

Comparatives vs. Superlatives

One of the key roles that modifiers play is to indicate how one thing compares to another. *He is tall* tells us only about his height in the absolute. The comparative form, *he is taller*, tells us that his height is greater than something or someone or a group of somethings or someones. The comparative form is used to compare two things. And the superlative form, *he is the tallest*, tells us that out of all the persons or things being considered, this guy is the overall winner on height. The trouble comes with certain modifiers for which we confuse the comparative and superlative forms. The following errors are the most common of this type.

36. Bigger vs. Biggest

Don't Say: Which of these two guys has the *biggest* feet?
Say Instead: Which of these two guys has the *bigger* feet?

Here's Why: When you're making a comparison between two things, you need to use the comparative form, and in this case, that's "bigger." If there had been more than two guys here, then you would have used the superlative form and said "which of these guys has the biggest feet?" Additional correct examples are:

127

Julie took the bigger piece of pie and left Stan to suffer with the sliver that was left.

Is that the biggest bubble you can blow?

Steve is the bigger of the two, but Jerry is the smarter.

The biggest mistake you ever made was thinking you could get your horse through that pond.

37. Less vs. Least

Don't Say: Of all the movies, that one seems *less* deserving of the award.

Say Instead: Of all the movies, that one seems *least* deserving of the award.

Here's Why: "Less" is the comparative form, so you can only use it when you're comparing two things. In this case, however, we begin by saying "of all the movies"—an indication that we're talking about more than two. So we need the superlative form, "least." Here are more correct examples:

You know you're in trouble when the lobster stuffed with caviar is the least expensive thing on the menu.

I like you less than I did yesterday.

Nothing she could say would make me the least bit interested in going back to her.

I'm less curious than you are about how the book ends.

38. Better vs. Best

Don't Say: The *best* of the two golfers actually lost the game.

Say Instead: The *better* of the two golfers actually lost the game.

Here's Why: Same principle with "less" and "least." "Better" is the comparative form, used for comparing two things. "Best" is the superlative, used for more than two. So in this sentence, when we know we're talking about two golfers, "better" is right. Additional correct examples are:

> If your brother won the spelling bee, what makes you think you're the <u>better</u> speller?
> Let her think she made the <u>best</u> pie ever.
> Here's the chess board, and may the <u>better</u> player win.
> Only the <u>best</u> writers are selected for the scholarship.

39. More vs. Most

Don't Say: I think he's *more smarter* when he's at the office.
Say Instead: I think he's *smarter* when he's at the office.

Here's Why: Many modifiers can be made comparative or superlative by adding an "-er" or an "-est" ending, as in *smart, smarter, smartest.* But you can also do the same job by using "more" or "most" in front of the modifier. "More" is the comparative, used when you're talking about only two things, and "most" is the superlative, used when something is being compared to a group. You must use "more" and "most" with modifiers that don't have "-er" and "-est" forms: You say *more intelligent* and *most intelligent,* not *intelligenter* or *intelligentest.* Conservative speakers believe that modifiers such as "smart" that do have "-er" and "-est" endings should never be mixed with "more" and "most"—it's always "smarter," and never "more smart." Some speakers are more relaxed about that rule, and permit "more" with words such as "smart" or "pretty." But the one thing you should never, ever do is add the "-er" or "-est" endings to a word that you're also modifying with "more" or "most": It's never "more smarter" or "most smartest." Then you have two words doing the same job. More correct examples are:

> She is the <u>prettiest</u> of all their children.
> She is the <u>most beautiful</u> of all their children.

This is the <u>most vicious</u> review I've ever read!
This is the <u>cruelest</u> review I've ever read!
His story was <u>shorter</u> than Tom's.
His story was <u>more interesting</u> than Tom's.

Test: Comparatives vs. Superlatives

Please circle the correct choice.

1. Both professors had published a book that week, so they spent the entire evening arguing over which book was (bigger, biggest).

2. Which of the Three Stooges has the (bigger, biggest) following among adolescent males?

3. Of all their six dogs, I think Fifi is (less, the least) likely to do something embarrassing in front of Aunt Nora.

4. Rolando couldn't decide between his two evil schemes; the first was (less, the least) difficult, but the second was (more, the most) fiendish.

5. Gloria will be (happier, more happier) when the kids are out of the house and she can play poker all day.

6. It was the (tastiest, most tastiest) anchovy-and-onion pizza they had ever eaten.

Answer Key: Comparatives vs. Superlatives

1. bigger.
2. biggest.
3. the least.
4. less, more.
5. happier.
6. tastiest.

Distance/Number/Quantity Modifiers

Another group of modifiers that seems to generate a lot of errors are modifiers of measurable distance, number, or quantity. Mistakes happen when the distinctions in meaning among some of them get blurred, as is the case with the following errors.

40. Between vs. Among

Don't Say: All right, I'll tell you, but it stays *between* us three, okay?
Say Instead: All right, I'll tell you, but it stays *among* us three, okay?

Here's Why: "Between" describes a relationship between two things only. "Among" is used when you're referring to more than two things, which is the case in this sentence. Additional correct examples are:

Among all the candidates, he was the smartest.
Sandy couldn't choose between the two job offers.

41. Fewer vs. Less

Don't Say: Tim has *less* projects than Nancy does.
Say Instead: Tim has *fewer* projects than Nancy does.

Here's Why: Strictly speaking, "less" refers to a quantity or an amount among things that cannot be counted or measured individually, including abstract ideas; and "fewer" refers to quantity among things that can be counted individually. In this case, where the number of Nancy and Tim's projects can be counted, "fewer" is the appropriate choice. Additional correct examples are:

She had no fewer than 11 bridesmaids at that wedding.
He is less well off than he was at the old job.

131

The <u>fewer</u> bills I have to pay, the better.
He took <u>less</u> credit for his work than he should have.

42. Farther vs. Further

Don't Say: You may be able to run *further*, but Mary can run faster.
Say Instead: You may be able to run *farther*, but Mary can run faster.

Here's Why: Many speakers use these terms interchangeably, and you probably won't get into trouble if you do, too. But conservative speakers argue that there's a meaningful distinction between them. "Farther" refers to measurable distance. "Further" refers to degree, quantity, time, or other qualities that are not being precisely measured. In this instance, we are talking about a measurable distance, how far one person can run compared to another, so "farther" is correct. Additional correct examples are:

Can you promise me there will be no <u>further</u> delays?
The map says the island is <u>farther</u> away than we thought.
We argued <u>further</u> about Terry after he had left.
He's out of the wheelchair and walking a little <u>farther</u> each day.

43. Number vs. Amount

Don't Say: Did you calculate the *amount* of pigs-in-a-blanket we'll need for the party?
Say Instead: Did you calculate the *number* of pigs-in-a-blanket we'll need for the party?

Here's Why: "Amount" refers to the specific mass, weight, size, or total parts of a tangible or intangible thing. It's not about things you count individually. That's where "number"

132

comes in. Here, where the question is how many pigs-in-a-blanket will be required to feed the lucky guests, "number" is the word we want. Additional correct examples are:

> The <u>amount</u> of food that boy eats every day is staggering.
> The <u>number</u> of errors on Eloise's tax return set a record.
> For what <u>amount</u> should Sue make out the check?
> There were a large <u>number</u> of people in line when we arrived at the movie.

44. So far as vs. As far as

> **Don't Say:** Her word is good, *as far as* I know.
> **Say Instead:** Her word is good, *so far as* I know.

Here's Why: "As far as" indicates a distance that could be measured if one were so inclined. "So far as" indicates a physical or conceptual distance that cannot be measured. In this sentence, it's impossible to measure the amount the speaker knows about how good the woman's word is. The phrase "so far as" is therefore correct. Other correct examples are:

> Are you taking the train <u>as far as</u> I am?
> <u>So far as</u> she can tell, Matt is unhappy with the arrangement.
> There were books <u>as far as</u> the eye could see.
> There were two pickpockets, <u>so far as</u> she remembers.

Test: Distance/Number/Quantity Modifiers

Please circle the correct choice.

1. (Between, among) you and (I, me), Rudolph isn't (real, really) smart.
2. Sometimes Imelda took hours to choose (between, among) her thousand pairs of shoes.

3. Our evening was (fewer, less) delightful than we'd planned.

4. We found (fewer, less) errors in the reports he wrote after he broke up with Margaret.

5. The (farther, further) he fled, the more diligently she pursued him.

6. If they pursue their discussions about the meaning of life any (farther, further), they'll get completely confused.

7. He seemed to enjoy the meal, but we found a large (number, amount) of Brussels sprouts hidden under his chair when he left.

8. We bought the (number, amount) of linoleum that would just cover the kitchen.

9. Broccoli, liver, leftover hash—how can we choose (between, among) such wonderful treats?

10. The (number, amount) of people willing to deal with you for any (number, amount) of time is decreasing rapidly.

11. The (fewer, less) he sees of her, the (fewer, less) panic attacks he has.

12. We won't get any (farther, further) by continuing this conversation.

13. Juliet boasted that she could go (farther, further) on her pogo stick than Frank—and do it in (fewer, less) time, too.

14. (Between, Among) my numerous acquaintances, Ronette is by far the best at picking locks.

15. They both look so cute that I can't possibly choose (between, among) them.

Answer Key: Distance/Number/Quantity Modifiers

1. Between, me, really. "Me" is the object of the preposition "between" (see Chapter 1).

2. among.

3. less.

4. fewer.

5. farther. (Preferred by more conservative speakers to express a measurable quantity such as physical distance.)

6. further. (Preferred by more conservative speakers to express a nonmeasurable amount.)

7. number.

8. amount.

9. among.

10. number, amount.

11. less, fewer.

12. further. (Preferred by more conservative speakers.)

13. farther (preferred by more conservative speakers), less.

14. Among.

15. between.

Absolute Modifiers

Another trap to watch out for is in the group of absolute modifiers. These are words that have only one shade of meaning: They're black and white. So putting another modifier in front of them that suggests degree, comparison, or limitation—such as "very" or "most"—is a no-no. The following sections include the most common errors of this type.

45. Unique vs. Most Unique

Don't Say: This is the *most unique* piece of art in the collection.
Say Instead: This piece of art is *unique*.

Here's Why: "Unique" means one of a kind. A thing cannot be more or less unique. And although something that is unique is unusual by definition, "unique" should not be used as a synonym for unusual. If what you mean is that there is no other piece like this one in the world, then "unique" is correct.

135

If you had meant that the piece was simply the most unusual one in the collection, then "most unusual" would have been appropriate.

46. Perfect vs. More Perfect

Don't Say: This date was *more perfect* than most.
Say Instead: This date was *perfect*.

Here's Why: Something that is truly perfect allows no comparison because perfection is an absolute. A thing has either achieved perfection or it hasn't, so it's impossible for one thing to be more perfect than another. In this case, if you mean the evening was truly perfect, then just say it was perfect. If, however, the important idea is that the date compares favorably to others, then say that it was better, or more exciting, or more romantic than most. And go out with that person again.

47. Infinite vs. Less Infinite

Don't Say: His patience is *less infinite* than hers.
Say Instead: His patience is not *infinite* the way hers is.

Here's Why: You're probably way ahead of us here. "Infinite" means that something is endless, without limits. It's impossible for one thing to be less endless than another, because a thing either has this quality or it does not. In this sentence, the idea is that her patience is infinite, and his patience is limited. The way we chose to correct the example sentence, *His patience is not infinite*, is only one option. We also could have said, *He lacks her infinite patience*, or, *Unlike her, he doesn't have infinite patience*, and so on.

Finally, here are two errors with absolute modifiers that involve not a logical impossibility, but a distinction between two similar states that aren't quite the same.

48. Ultimate vs. Penultimate

Don't Say: He gave Sydney a raise, the *penultimate* compliment.
Say Instead: He gave Sydney a raise, the *ultimate* compliment.

Here's Why: The word "penultimate" doesn't mean "something beyond the ultimate," instead, it means "next to the last in a series" or "the one before or lesser than the ultimate." If ultimate is first prize, then penultimate is second prize: just the opposite of what many people take it to mean. For the curious, there's an even fancier word, "antepenultimate," that means "the one before the one before the ultimate": third prize, if you want to stick to the previous metaphor. Neither "antepenultimate" nor "penultimate" are words you need all that often, and they certainly don't refer to state of perfection surpassing the ultimate. So in this sentence, unless you mean to say that the compliment of the raise was secondary to some other, ultimate, compliment (chocolate, perhaps? a weekend in the Bahamas?) just say "ultimate."

49. Pregnant vs. Less Pregnant

Don't Say: My sister is *less pregnant* than she looks.
Say Instead: My sister is *less far along in her pregnancy* than she looks.

Here's Why: Speakers differ on this one. Conservative speakers argue that a woman is either pregnant or not pregnant, so it doesn't make sense to modify "pregnant" with modifiers such as "less," "more," or "very." But less conservative speakers argue that being pregnant, unlike being perfect or being unique, is a process with a beginning, middle, and end, and that modifiers of degree can help indicate where a woman is in this process. We might not condemn passengers on a crowded bus who *didn't offer a seat to a pregnant woman* (after all, at some points in a pregnancy, some women can comfortably run a marathon), but we might get a bit peeved at passengers who *didn't offer a seat to an extremely pregnant woman*. Unlike the case of "most unique" or "more perfect," then, the modifier here is not illogical and conveys useful information.

It's your call on this one: "very pregnant" is one of those expressions (like "hopefully," which we'll tell you about shortly) that self-appointed members of the Language Police love to correct in others. So to be on the safe side, you should use modifiers with "pregnant" only when the meaning of the sentence absolutely requires you to mark off parts of the process. And avoid modifiers with "pregnant" altogether in very formal speech or writing.

Test: Absolute Modifiers

Please circle the correct choice.

1. Aunt Flora had some interesting clothes, but her penguin feather boa was (unique, the most unique).

2. Larry was justly proud of his pompadour, which had been declared by a jury of distinguished Elvis impersonators to be (perfect, the most perfect).

3. My list of things to do is (less infinite than it was yesterday, not infinite as it was yesterday).

4. (Pregnant, Very pregnant) women should not eat or drink anything that might harm the baby.

5. The wallpaper in the nursery looks wonderful, which is a miracle considering that I had to put it up when I was (pregnant, very pregnant).

6. Three arguments led to their breakup. The first argument was about politics; the (ultimate, penultimate) argument concerned who should walk the dog, and the (ultimate, penultimate) brawl came when he used her collection of antique salad tongs for firewood.

138

Answer Key: Absolute Modifiers

1. unique.

2. perfect.

3. not infinite as it was yesterday.

4. pregnant. This sentence refers to something that all pregnant women should do, no matter what the stage of the pregnancy.

5. very pregnant. While conservative speakers believe that "pregnant" should not be qualified, pregnancy does have a beginning, middle, and end, and it is notably more difficult to put up wallpaper at the end. For less conservative speakers, "very" is appropriate here.

6. penultimate, ultimate.

Imprecise and Made-up Modifiers

50. Hopefully

Don't Say: *Hopefully*, Leslie will remember to pick up the pig at the vet's.
Say Instead: *I hope* Leslie will remember to pick up the pig at the vet's.

Here's Why: Remember the Language Police from the section on "pregnant"? Well, they really get worked up about "hopefully," too. The intent in our error sentence is to use "hopefully" to convey the speaker's feelings about the whole sentence: I hope that such-and-such will happen. The Language Police argue that we can't use an adverb to modify a whole sentence in this way: An adverb can only modify a verb, an adjective, or another adverb. A correct use of "hopefully" restricted to normal adverbial duty would be *Jim waited hopefully by the phone*, meaning that Jim is sitting by the phone full of hope. If that's what "hopefully" is doing here, then the sentence would mean that Leslie's action of remembering to pick up the pig will be carried out by her in a hopeful manner—and, of course, that's not what we really want to say here.

On the other hand, not only is the broader use of "hopefully" common—so common that no one will have difficulty understanding you—but it's grammatically identical to other adverbs that don't raise such a ruckus. "Frankly," for example, is often used to convey the speaker's feelings about a sentence: *Frankly, that pig eats so much that there's not enough food left for the children.* No one would dream that you meant to say that the pig was eating in a frank manner; the adverb quite clearly relates to the speaker's feelings, just like "hopefully" often does in casual usage. But because many people still interpret the "incorrect" use of "hopefully" as an error, you may want to play it safe on this one, and substitute "I hope that" or "If things work out" or "If the gods smile on us, Leslie will remember that pig."

51. Regretfully

> **Don't Say:** *Regretfully,* we can't be in town for your party.
> **Say Instead:** *I'm sorry that* we can't be in town for your party.

Here's Why: Here's another favorite of the Language Police. Like "hopefully," "regretfully" (they argue) is an adverb meaning "in a regretful manner." It shouldn't be used as a substitute for "I regret that" or "I'm sorry that" or "unfortunately." It's all right to say *I must regretfully decline your invitation,* because declining is something that can be done in a regretful manner. But to say *regretfully, we can't be in town* is technically to say that these people cannot be in town in a state of regret.

52. Awful

> **Don't Say:** That suit looks *awful* on you
> **Say Instead:** That suit looks *terrible* on you.

Here's Why: No one's going to throw you in jail for this one, but it's good to know when you want to be extra-impressive: "Awful" is an adjective meaning, in its truest sense, "awe-inspiring." There are still some around who would argue that it is incorrect to use "awful" when you mean "bad." Unfortunately, it's hard to know just who these people are—you'll have to decide if you want to live dangerously on this one.

53. Plenty

> **Don't Say:** That music of yours is *plenty* loud.
> **Say Instead:** That music of yours is *very* loud.

Here's Why: "Plenty" may be used only as a noun or an adjective in standard English, as in *plenty of money* and *they had plenty*. Using it as an adverb—as a substitute for "very"—is out of bounds, unless maybe you're a novelist whose characters don't know any better.

Test: Imprecise and Made-up Modifiers

Please rewrite the following sentences, replacing the words in italics with more precise modifiers.

1. *Hopefully*, Hector will be able to defuse the bomb in time.
2. *Regretfully*, the woodchucks have eaten your prize petunias.
3. I know this hat is *awful*, but at least I bought it on sale.
4. You look *plenty* cute in those fuzzy slippers.

Answer Key: Imprecise and Made-up Modifiers

1. <u>I hope that</u> Hector will be able to defuse the bomb in time.
2. <u>I'm sorry that</u> the woodchucks have eaten your prize petunias.
3. I know this hat is <u>terrible</u> *or* <u>ugly</u> *or* <u>vile</u>, but at least I bought it on sale.
4. You look <u>very</u> *or* <u>really</u> cute in those fuzzy slippers.

Problem Preposition

As a class, prepositions tend to be pretty agreeable. They go where they're told and do what's asked of them. But they are persnickety on a few points, such as how and when they are to be paired up with a given verb, whether or not they feel like hanging out alone at the end of a sentence, and how to get other parts of speech to stop barging in on their territory. The following entries represent the most common errors made with prepositions.

Prepositions Expressing Fine Shades of Meaning

54. Agree to vs. Agree with

Don't Say: Are you saying you *agree to* their arguments?
Say Instead: Are you saying you *agree with* their arguments?

Here's Why: How do you know whether to use "to" or "with"? "Agree to" introduces an infinitive form of a verb such as "to jump," "to suppose," or "to annoy." It means to consent

143

to, as in consenting to fulfill the terms of a contract. "Agree with" introduces a noun. It means to be in accord or alignment with, as in agreeing with a point of view. So in this sentence, where we don't have an infinitive, and where we're talking about being on the same side in an argument, "agree with" is correct. Additional correct examples are:

> Joe agreed to stay if Aunt Fannie would let him have the dark meat.
> I agree with you, but that doesn't mean I like you.
> We knew they were too naïve to get married when they agreed to obey each other.
> She has always agreed with his philosophy on work.

55. Differ with vs. Differ from

Don't Say: We *differed from* the Trumbles on their right to park their cars on our front lawn.
Say Instead: We *differed with* the Trumbles on their right to park their cars on our front lawn.

Here's Why: "Differ from" means to be unlike, as in one dress differing from another. "Differ with" means to disagree with, as in differing with a point of view, which is the case in our example sentence. Additional examples are:

> You can differ with me without getting huffy about it.
> Only their parents can tell how the twins differ from one another.
> The two sides differed with each other on several points but finally worked out an agreement.
> How do you do differ from your predecessor?

56. Different from vs. Different than

Don't Say: Hey, my invitation looks *different than* hers.
Say Instead: Hey, my invitation looks *different from* hers.

Here's Why: "Different from" is standard, always acceptable. But there is a range of opinions from usage experts on the appropriateness of "different than." "Different than" is acceptable to less conservative speakers when it is followed by a clause, as in *I felt different than I did the last time I took this medication*. (More conservative speakers veto "different than" altogether, and would rephrase such a sentence so that "different from" would be followed by a noun or pronoun.) What's never a good idea is using "different than" when making a quick, straightforward comparison between two persons or things, as we did in our example. In other words, don't say *A is different than B*. Additional correct examples are:

His style is <u>different from</u> hers.

Will you take a <u>different</u> route <u>than</u> the one you took the last time you went there?

Can you tell if this engraving is <u>different from</u> that one?

Test: Prepositions Expressing Fine Shades of Meaning

Please circle the correct choice.

1. Elvira reluctantly (agreed to, agreed with) knit booties for all the quintuplets.

2. Unfortunately the cannibals did not (agree to, agree with) Fred's theory that eating people is wrong.

3. We would have gotten along splendidly if we didn't (differ with, differ from) each other on all philosophical, moral, and political questions.

4. His account of the 12-car pile-up was (different from, different than) hers.

5. She gave a very different account (than, from) he did of the 12-car pile-up.

6. When Zelda recovered from the effects of the champagne, she found she had married a man (different than, different from) her fiancé.

7. Is this tie really (different than, different from) the one you gave me last year?

Answer Key:
Prepositions That Express Fine Shades of Meaning

1. agreed to.
2. agree with.
3. differ with. Don't forget that "differ from" is correct when you're comparing physical qualities rather than opinions. The following example is correct: *Horace was chagrined to discover that his $500 radio hardly differed from the cheap knockoff his brother had bought at a flea market.*
4. different from.
5. different than. More conservative speakers believe that "different than" should never be used. In a case like this one, a conservative speaker would first rephrase the sentence so that it makes a quick comparison, and then use "different from": *His account of the 12-car pile-up was different from the one that she gave.*
6. different from.
7. different from.

Unidiomatic and Superfluous Prepositions

57. Centers around

Don't Say: Their problem *centers around* the fact that his business is failing.
Say Instead: Their problem *centers on* the fact that his business is failing.

Here's Why: It is impossible for anything to "center around." A center is the exact middle of something, so by

146

definition it cannot be around anything else—it would no longer be the center. A thing can center on or in something else, it can be centered by something else, but it can never be centered around.

58. Where…At

Don't Say: Where are they *at*?
Say Instead: Where are they?

Here's Why: The preposition "at" is always unnecessary with "where." It performs the same job in the sentence by referring to location, which is what the "where" is there for in the first place. The use of "at" in this way is not uncommon, but it is a big tip-off to others that you're careless.

59. As to

Don't Say: I accepted the diamond necklace as a gift without inquiring *as to* its history.
Say Instead: I accepted the diamond necklace as a gift without inquiring *about* its history.

Here's Why: Usage experts aren't unanimous on this one, but there is a widespread belief that the phrase "as to" is more often than not pretentious-sounding clutter. "As to" does have appropriate uses, such as when you want to begin a sentence by putting a lot of emphasis on a word or phrase that would otherwise have to come later. For example: *As to his health, we did not inquire for fear of angering him.* Or: *As to your decision on the highway project, I cannot agree with you.* The kind of use of "as to" that is usually frowned on is employing it as a substitute for prepositions—a use that seems irresistible to folks who are trying to sound businesslike or formal but which generally ends up having the opposite effect. The following are some more examples of "as to" replacing a preposition, each paired with a preferred version (note that there is more than one way to improve these; only one option has been selected).

Instead of His opinions <u>as to</u> her character, *say* His opinions <u>on</u> her character.

Instead of The meeting <u>as to</u> which O'Brien was called, *say* The meeting <u>to</u> which O'Brien was called.

Instead of We're deciding <u>as to</u> the future goals of the committee, *say* We're deciding <u>upon</u> the future goals of the committee.

60. Off of

Don't Say: When he gets *off of* his soapbox, maybe we can get some work done.
Say Instead: When he gets *off* his soapbox, maybe we can get some work done.

Here's Why: You don't need the "of" after off, the way you would after some other prepositions such as "out," as in *he got <u>out of</u> the car*. When you're using "off" simply say *he got <u>off</u> the bus*, and leave it at that.

61. Over with

Don't Say: Is the meeting *over with*?
Say Instead: Is the meeting *over*?

Here's Why: "Over with" is an informal phrase that expresses an intense desire to complete an unpleasant task. If that's what you mean, go ahead and say it, as in *Let's get this over with* or *Isn't Bob's recitation of his five-book epic poem over with yet?* But if you're simply referring to something as being finished, as is the case with the meeting here, then stick to "over" by itself.

62. Type of a

Don't Say: Hey, what *type of a* place are you running here?

Say Instead: Hey, what *type of* place are you running here?

Here's Why: When using the phrase "type of," the extra "a" is always unnecessary and incorrect. Just say *type of job*, *type of flower*, *type of lipstick*, plain and simple.

Test: Unidiomatic and Superfluous Prepositions

Please circle the correct choice.

1. Maurice's whole life (centers on, centers around) caring for his prize cactus.

2. Rex drove around for hours because he was too embarrassed to ask anyone where the Shyness Clinic (was, was at).

3. I refuse to start cooking until you get that cat (off, off of) the kitchen counter.

4. I am writing to inform you (as to, about) the goals of our new 25-year budget plan.

5. Well, thank goodness that's (over, over with)—I thought the speech would never end.

6. I'll help you with your algebra homework as soon as my favorite TV program is (over, over with).

7. What (type of, type of a) question is that?

Answer Key:
Unidiomatic and Superfluous Prepositions

1. centers on.
2. was.
3. off.

4. about.

5. over with. Here, the speaker clearly awaits the end of the speech with great eagerness, so the intensifier "with" is appropriate.

6. over. Here, the speaker is matter-of-factly referring to the end of a TV program, and not to something that seems unbearably long, so "over" is appropriate.

7. type of.

Confused Connections

In this chapter we'll look at words we use to link parts of sentences together, words such as "and" and "because." They're called **connectors** or **conjunctions** in the grammar trade, and most of them aren't too hard to handle. You can use connectors such as "and" and "or" to establish a simple link, such as, *I cleaned out the bathroom and threw out the trash this afternoon.* Here "and" is just a time-saver: It allows you to list everything you did this afternoon without having to stop and say two different sentences. But other connectors such as "because" and "therefore" have a more exciting job: They make a *logical* link between two thoughts: *I deserve an extra slice of pie because I cleaned out the bathroom and threw out the trash this afternoon.* Here the connector lets people know you're about to give a reason for what you're doing (not necessarily a *good* reason, but that's not the connector's fault).

Most connectors are cooperative little words that work hard in their sentences and don't make trouble. But two kinds of connectors can sometimes get confusing: two-part connectors we call "bookend expressions," and imprecise connectors that just don't get the right idea across. Let's take them one at a time.

Bookend Expressions

This section could properly be called "Problems With Correlative Conjunctions," but then you might have skipped it out of terror, and it's not really that tricky. Correlative conjunctions are simply pairs of words that join together other phrases. For example, the sentence *Either you take your feet off the table or I'll take them off for you* features a famous pair, "either/or." The difficulties people have with these connectors tend to be of two types. Type one: leaving out the second half of the conjunction. Type two: choosing a second half that is not the proper mate for the first half. Thinking of correlative conjunctions as bookends is helpful because these expressions, properly paired, give a kind of order and structure to the string of words in a sentence. And if you leave one off, or try to partner a bookend with something weaker than its true mate, things get sloppy fast, and before you know it, you have a spill. The following sections contain the most common errors made with bookend expressions.

63. Not only...But/But also

Don't Say: He is *not only* too big for the kiddie pool, he is too scary in that snorkeling gear.

Say Instead: He is *not only* too big for the kiddie pool, *but also* too scary in that snorkeling gear.

Here's Why: Whenever you use "not only" to introduce one part of a two-part idea, you need to complete the thought by introducing the second part with "but" or "but also." Simple. Here are more correct examples of this pair of bookends in action:

Jane is <u>not only</u> brilliant, <u>but</u> charming.
<u>Not only</u> will I dock your pay, <u>but</u> I will <u>also</u> put you on notice.

They <u>not only</u> showed up uninvited, <u>but also</u> brought cheap wine.

His answer revealed <u>not only</u> his love for the game, <u>but also</u> his commitment to this losing team.

64. On the one hand...On the other hand

Don't Say: *On the one hand*, Mitch is good looking, but then he's never much fun to talk to.
Say Instead: *On the one hand*, Mitch is good looking, but *on the other hand*, he's never much fun to talk to.

Here's Why: You need both "hands" to be organized and tidy in sentences such as these. The whole idea is to compare two opposite points, as we're trying to do here with the attractive, but boring, Mitch. So the minute you hear *on the one hand* coming out of your mouth, get ready to introduce the flip side with *on the other hand*. You can drop the second "hand," and say *on the one hand...on the other*, but you don't get to substitute entirely new phrases such as "but then" or "only then" or "except that." A few more correct examples are:

She is, <u>on the one hand</u>, a stunning performer, and, <u>on the other hand</u>, a terror to deal with backstage.
<u>On the one hand</u>, we could go to your mother's, but <u>on the other</u>, we could just invite her here.
You could see that, <u>on the one hand,</u> they wanted to get married, but, <u>on the other hand</u>, they were petrified.

One final note on this expression: You can only use it to compare two things, because you only have two hands! So unless you belong to an alien race of three-handed Martians, don't say *On the one hand, we could go to the beach; on the other hand, we could go to the mall; on the other hand, we could just stay home and play canasta.* Instead, sort out your alternatives so you're only using two hands: *On the one*

153

hand, we could go to the beach or the mall, but on the other hand, we could just stay home and play canasta.

65. Either...Or

> **Don't Say:** You *either* answer my question *or else* go to your room.
> **Say Instead:** You *either* answer my question *or* go to your room.

Here's Why: Most people remember to follow "either" with "or," but sometimes we throw in other words that add nothing and just muck up the sentence. So avoid "or else" and "or maybe" and such phrases when you're using "either/or."

66. Neither...Nor

> **Don't Say:** He's not going to school or working, *neither*.
> **Say Instead:** He's *neither* going to school *nor* working.

Here's Why: You never get to have a "neither" without a "nor" when your intention is to compare two things, as it is in this sentence. You can use "neither" as a pronoun, as in *He invited <u>neither</u> of them.* But if you were to revise that sentence to use "neither" as a conjunction, you'd need "nor" as follows: *He invited <u>neither</u> John <u>nor</u> Sarah.*

67. As...As

> **Don't Say:** *As* surely *that* this is payday, she'll be at the racetrack.
> **Say Instead:** *As* surely *as* this is payday, she'll be at the racetrack.

Here's Why: When you use "as" to begin this type of comparison, you need another "as" to follow up, not another word such as "that." Here are some more examples:

As guilty as he looks, he'll surely be convicted.
She did as poorly on the test as Mary.
She looked surprisingly calm, as harrowing as the trek
had been.

68. The reason...Was that

> **Don't Say:** *The reason* Jay survived *was because* he had
> packed a case of chocolate bars for the journey.
> **Say Instead:** *The reason* Jay survived *was that* he had
> packed a case of chocolate bars for the journey.

Here's Why: Once you say, "the reason," you've told your
listeners that you're talking about a cause-and-effect relationship between two things. All that's left for you is to say that the
reason was this or that. Saying *the reason was because* is
redundant—"because" is just another way of saying, "the reason." Additional correct examples that illustrate the difference
between constructions with "the reason" and "because":

The reason Emily came dressed as Helen of Troy was
that she'd been told it was a costume party.
Emily came as Helen of Troy because she'd been told
it was a costume party.
Mulligan said the reason he is serving is that the head
waiter is sick.
Mulligan is serving because the head waiter is sick.

Test: Bookend Expressions

Please use *not only/but, also* to link the following
sentences.

1. Her date is boring. Her date is ugly.
2. I will give you unconditional love. I will do your laundry.
3. Stanley hated the party because the guests were all too
   rowdy. He spilled Tabasco sauce on his favorite tie.

Please use *on the one hand/on the other hand* to link the following sentences.

4. We were exhausted and would take weeks to recover from our injuries. We'd sure had a good time.

5. Al is smart. Al is conceited. Al is good with children.

Please circle the correct choice.

6. You can either look it up in the dictionary (or, or maybe) ask your mother what it means.

7. The screwdriver is neither in the toolbox where it should be (or, nor) under the sink where you left it.

8. You must either do exactly what I say (or, or else) face dire consequences.

9. As thrilling (as, that) the roller coaster was, Frank was relieved that Tracy didn't want to ride it for an eighth time.

Correct the following sentences.

10. You can't holler down my rain barrel or climb my apple tree, neither.

11. The reason he couldn't sleep is because he couldn't stop thinking about Angela.

Answer Key: Bookend Expressions

1. Her date is <u>not only</u> boring, <u>but</u> ugly.

2. I will <u>not only</u> give you unconditional love, <u>but also</u> do your laundry.

3. Stanley hated the party <u>not only</u> because the guests were all too rowdy, <u>but also</u> because he spilled Tabasco sauce on his favorite tie.

4. <u>On the one hand</u>, we were exhausted and would take weeks to recover from our injuries, <u>but on the other hand</u>, we'd sure had a good time.

5. <u>On the one hand</u>, Al is smart and good with children, <u>but on the other hand</u>, he's conceited.

To emphasize the good side of Al's character, you can reverse the order of the clauses: *On the one hand, Al is conceited, but on the other hand, he's smart and good with children.* What you can't do is give each of Al's three qualities a hand. The following revision is incorrect: *On the one hand, Al is conceited, but on the other hand, he's smart, but on the other hand* (the third hand!?) *he's good with children.*

6. or.

7. nor.

8. or.

9. as.

10. You can <u>neither</u> holler down my rain barrel <u>nor</u> climb my apple tree.

11. <u>The reason</u> he couldn't sleep is <u>that</u> he couldn't stop thinking about Angela.

    Or: He couldn't sleep <u>because</u> he couldn't stop thinking about Angela.

Imprecise, Pretentious, or Needless Connectors

These errors include connectors that just don't say quite what we want them to say. They're not grammatically incorrect, but they're fuzzy, and they make our speech sound less clear and direct than it should be. The following are some of the most common fuzzballs of the bunch.

69. Where

Don't Say: A home run is *where* the batter hits the ball out of the park.

Say Instead: A home run *means that* the batter has hit the ball out of the park.

Here's Why: "Where" can be a lot of things—an adverb, a conjunction, or a noun—but one role it should not play in standard English is that of introducing a noun clause the way it does in the example. When you're defining or naming something, as we are in this example, "where" is a no-no.

70. Per

> **Don't Say**: *Per* your request, we'll send the materials this Friday.
> **Say Instead:** *As you requested*, we'll send the materials this Friday.

Here's Why: Ah, business jargon. "Per" may make you feel like you're really saying something important, but unfortunately, it's the fuzziest of fuzzy connectors. The appropriate use of "per" is restricted to the prepositional, in a description of ratios such as *30 miles per gallon*. In business situations, people often throw it in as a kind of an all-purpose connector. It can mean "according to" (*Per the report, the project is five days ahead of schedule*) or it can mean "to comply with" (*We have changed the procedures per your instructions*). The problem here is that no one will know quite what you mean—or worse, they'll assume you mean one thing when, in fact, you mean quite another.

Also—to those in the know—using "per" can make you look as if you're trying too hard—using a fancy (but imprecise) word where another one would be more appropriate. Avoid "per"!

71. Plus

> **Don't Say:** The place is hard to get to, *plus* the food is bad.
> **Say Instead:** The place is hard to get to, *and* the food is bad.

Here's Why: The use of "plus" to join two clauses as a replacement for "and" is nonstandard. You may say, *two plus two is four*. You may even say, *The effects of the heat plus the humidity were too much for her*, because you're staying inside one clause to join two nouns together. But not if you're assembling entire clauses, and you mean "besides," as we did in this example with the food at the restaurant.

72. As to whether

Don't Say: Nellie doubted *as to whether* the fly swatter could be used in that way.
Say Instead: Nellie doubted *whether* the fly swatter could be used in that way.

Here's Why: Most of the time, "as to" is just unnecessary fluff before the word "whether." Watch how the following phrases are nicely streamlined by taking out the "as to"s:

Instead of Deciding as to whether we should buy the house, *say* Deciding whether we should buy the house.
Instead of Guessing as to whether she'll show up, *say* Guessing whether she'll show up.
Instead of No longer wondering as to whether he'd get a raise, *say* No longer wondering whether he'd get a raise.

73. In the event that

Don't Say: We'll take up that issue again *in the event that* interest rates decline.
Say Instead: We'll take up that issue again *if* interest rates decline.

Here's Why: "In the event that" is a cumbersome, flowery substitute for the word "if." So just say "if"!

159

74. Owing to the fact that

Don't Say: *Owing to the fact that* my paycheck is late, my rent check is going to be late, too.
Say Instead: *Because* my paycheck is late, my rent check is going to be late, too.

Here's Why: Again, it's not necessary to get so complicated about a simple idea. "Owing to the fact that" are just extra words and added awkwardness, so avoid this phrase.

75. As vs. Because/Since

Don't Say: *As* Lou looked engrossed in the phone book, Lisa didn't want to interrupt.
Say Instead: *Because* Lou looked engrossed in the phone book, Lisa didn't want to interrupt.

Here's Why: In most circumstances, "as" is a weak substitute for "because" and "since." One of the reasons this is true is that "as" also means "while." In the sentence above, it is unclear whether Lisa didn't want to interrupt *while* Lou was reading or *because* he was reading—two different meanings. If you choose either "because" or "since" instead of "as," you can't go wrong.

Test: Imprecise Conjunctions and Connectors

Please circle the correct answer.

1. Why am I screaming? I'm screaming (as, because) you're standing on my foot.
2. The window broke (as, because) Jim hurled a bowling ball through it.

The following sentences contain connecting words and phrases that aren't quite precise enough to convey the intended meaning. Try rewriting them, replacing the words in italics with more precise connectors. There are several ways to do each one; one or more possible revisions are suggested in the Answer Key.

3. Total disk failure *is where* all the data on your computer turns into gloop.

4. An aria *is where* the fat lady starts singing.

5. I've filled out the application for a goldfish license in triplicate and had it notarized *per* your instructions.

6. He hasn't done his laundry in months, *plus* his beard needs trimming.

7. *Per* the fire code, building repairs will be made by March 31.

8. *Per* your letter of the 12th, no action has been taken at this time.

9. They spent 45 minutes debating *as to whether* they should go to the concert in the rain.

10. *In the event that* she says yes, you'll have to pay for a ring somehow.

11. I can't give you my homework *due to the fact that* I haven't done it yet.

12. *Owing to the fact that* my car broke down, you'll have to chauffeur me this week.

Answer Key: Imprecise Conjunctions and Connectors

1. because.

2. because.

3. Total disk failure <u>means that</u> all the data on your computer turns into gloop.

   Or: Total disk failure <u>occurs when</u> all the data on your computer turns into gloop.

4. An aria <u>means that</u> the fat lady starts singing.

5. I've filled out the application for a goldfish license in triplicate and had it notarized <u>as you instructed</u>.

6. He hasn't done his laundry in months, <u>and</u> his beard needs trimming.

   Or for greater emphasis: He hasn't done his laundry in months, <u>and furthermore</u>, his beard needs trimming.

7. <u>To comply with</u> the fire code, building repairs will be made by March 31.

8. This one's tricky, and shows just how vague "per" can be. What did the writer really intend?

   <u>In response to</u> your letter of the 12th, no action has been taken at this time.

   <u>As you asked</u> in your letter of the 12th, no action has been taken at this time.

   <u>As we said</u> in our letter to you dated the 12th, no action has been taken at this time.

   To avoid this kind of confusing mess, avoid per!

9. They spent 45 minutes debating <u>whether</u> they should go to the concert.

10. <u>If</u> she says yes, you'll have to pay for a ring somehow.

11. I can't give you my homework <u>because</u> I haven't done it yet.

12. <u>Because</u> my car broke down, you'll have to chauffeur me this week.

Puzzling Plurals

CHAPTER 7

We do a good job using the correct singular and plural forms of most nouns, because the process isn't tricky; you just add an "s" or an "es" or an "ies" to make the plural form. But a few words that come to us from Latin and Greek don't follow the normal pattern. As a result, their singular and plural forms are often confused or unknown.

76. Media

> **Don't Say:** The media *is* protected by the first amendment.
> **Say Instead:** The media *are* protected by the first amendment.

Here's Why: It hardly seems fair that a dead language causes trouble for us in English. "Media" is plural, of Latin origin, referring to a *group* of vehicles through which ideas are communicated. The singular form is "medium." So in the example sentence, when we use the plural form "media," we need to follow it up with the plural verb "are" instead of the singular one, "is." There is one case in which many usage experts are comfortable treating "media" as singular, and that is when the group of vehicles is being referred to as a collective, as in *The media has become an institution just like the government*. However, you can avoid having to figure out whether a singular sense is acceptable or not simply by treating "media" as plural in every case—then you'll always be correct. Conversely, when you're referring to just one of the vehicles through which communication happens, remember to use the singular form, "medium." Here are some correct examples of each:

> His preferred <u>medium has been</u> newspapers, but I hear he's interested in television now.
> His preferred <u>media have been</u> newspapers and magazines.
> The <u>media work</u> overtime when there's a big story.
> The artist's <u>medium was</u> pen and ink.
> The artist works in mixed <u>media</u>.

There has been a trend lately toward making a plural out of the word "medium" by simply adding an "s" to get "mediums." One sees this in print from a range of sources, some downright respectable. For example, you might read, *He used several mediums to reach his audience.* However, this is a recent trend, and most well-spoken folks have been carefully educated that "media" is the plural of "medium." So you would be better off sticking to that traditional distinction if you want to be sure that your listeners or readers know you know what's right.

77. Data

> **Don't Say:** The data *shows* our plans have failed.
> **Say Instead:** The data *show* our plans have failed.

Here's Why: "Data" and "datum" work just like "media" and "medium." The "a" ending is plural; the "um" ending is singular. The only difference between the two examples may be this: The use of "data" as a singular goes down a little easier with usage experts than the use of "media" as a singular. And that's because facts often seem to travel in packs—so scientists and researchers typically think of data as a collective term. The bottom line is this: You'll always be correct if you treat data as a plural. But when your meaning is focused more on the string of facts taken together as a group, using "data" with a singular verb won't get you thrown in jail. It's a judgment call. Here are additional correct examples of the plural sense of "data":

The <u>data are</u> inconclusive, so we'll need another study.
The <u>data indicate</u> that Ellen's hypothesis was right.
The new <u>data make</u> the previous research obsolete.

78. Alumni

> **Don't Say:** Jim and Judy are both Michigan *alumnis*.
> **Say Instead:** Jim and Judy are both Michigan *alumni*.

Here's Why: Another term from Latin: This one has several forms you should know. One male graduate is an "alumnus." Two or more male graduates are "alumni," pronounced with a long "i," and never, ever, with an "s" at the end, as in the incorrect example. Two or more graduates of different sexes are also called "alumni," as in our corrected example. One female graduate is called an "alumna," and two female graduates are referred to as "alumnae," spelled with an "ae" at the end, but rhyming with "knee." An example of each are:

Geraldine is an <u>alumna</u> of Grinnell College.
Lucy and Beth are Sarah Lawrence <u>alumnae</u>.
Don is an <u>alumnus</u> of Lincoln High.
Joe and Fred are <u>alumni</u> but they don't donate money to the school.
Stacy and John are both <u>alumni</u>, but she's the only one going to the reunion.

165

79. Criteria

> **Don't Say:** Sense of humor was her only *criteria* in choosing a man.
>
> **Say Instead:** Sense of humor was her only *criterion* in choosing a man.

Here's Why: "Criteria" is the plural of "criterion," a word of Greek origin that means "standard" or "measure." In this sentence, the woman has only one measure by which she judges men acceptable or not, so we should use the singular "criterion," and wish her the best of luck. Separately, remember to use a plural verb whenever "criteria" is your subject. For example, it's *the criteria are* and not *the criteria is*. Additional correct examples are:

The snooty club's board of directors established a list of 60 criteria for membership.

He's such a simple man that his criterion for happiness is having enough ice for his soda.

Julie asked what the opera company's criteria were for screening chorus members.

Is looking good in red really a fair criterion for this job?

80. Phenomena

> **Don't Say:** Incredible *phenomenons* happen all around us every day if you know where to look.
>
> **Say Instead:** Incredible *phenomena* happen all around us every day if you know where to look.

Here's Why: "Phenomenon," which also comes to us from Greek, means an event that is observed through the senses rather than by thought. The plural form is "phenomena" not "phenomenons."

166

81. Memoranda

Don't Say: I typed *memorandums* today until my fingers cramped up.
Say Instead: I typed *memoranda* today until my fingers cramped up.

Here's Why: Okay, so you probably don't use the full word every day; you just say "memo" or "memos" instead. And that's fine. But when you do use the full word, remember that the plural form of "memorandum" is not "memorandums," it's "memoranda."

Test: Puzzling Plurals

Please circle the correct choice.

1. The mayor responded to the charges by complaining that the media (was, were) ganging up on her.

2. Our consumer preference data (reveal, reveals) that almost no one would buy a cereal called "Mothball Crunch."

3. Buffy and Babs, who are (alumnis, alumni, alumnae, alums) of a fine finishing school, have joined a motorcycle gang.

4. Yes, Donald and Ivana are (alumnis, alumni, alumnae, alums), but they've never given the school a dime.

5. To get insurance from that company you must meet two simple (criterion, criterions, criteria): you can't have an accident on your record, and you must promise never to have one.

6. The algebra teacher's only (criterion, criterions, criteria) for giving an A was perfect punctuation.

7. Toby came to work on time today for the first time ever; do you know the reason for this extraordinary (phenomenon, phenomenons, phenomena)?

8. Frogs have been falling from the sky and the sun has been rising in the west, but the scientists can't explain these unusual (phenomenon, phenomenons, phenomena).

9. Bill sends her several irate (memorandum, memoranda) each week on her habit of using his coffee mug as a planter.

Answer Key: Puzzling Plurals

1. were. (Plural)

2. reveal. (Plural)

3. More conservative speakers would use "alumnae" to refer to two female graduates; some less conservative speakers prefer "alums" as a gender-neutral plural.

4. More conservative speakers would use "alumni" here to refer to two graduates of different genders; some less conservative speakers prefer "alums" as a gender-neutral plural.

5. criteria. (Plural)

6. criterion. (Singular)

7. phenomenon. (Singular)

8. phenomena. (Plural)

9. memoranda. (Plural; "memos" is almost always also appropriate here for all but the most conservative speakers.)

Mixing up Words That Sound the Same

CHAPTER 8

One of the great things about the English language is its extraordinary depth. It has so many words that there seems to be one assigned to every possible sliver of an idea; every shade or nuance of meaning is covered. The difficulty with this, however, is that many of these nuances escape us, and we mistake one word for another—we make usage errors. In the next three chapters, we'll take a magnifying glass to pairs of words that are often confused and identify their precise meanings so that you'll know when and how to use them correctly.

This chapter will consider words that we mix up because they sound almost the same. One little letter can make a big difference!

82. Accept vs. Except

> **Don't Say:** All the men wore ties *accept* for Louis.
> **Say Instead:** All the men wore ties *except* for Louis.

Here's Why: "Accept" means to receive something or to agree to it as valid. "Except" means to exclude. In this sentence we are talking about excluding Louis from the group of men who wore ties, not receiving him, so "except" is correct. Additional correct examples are:

We accept your invitation.
Sally accepted all the applause.
Jerry came with all his former wives, except Marie.
Stuart was excepted from the meeting because he couldn't be trusted.

83. Advice vs. Advise

> **Don't Say:** My *advise* to you is to stop eating Maureen's Irish chili.
> **Say Instead:** My *advice* to you is to stop eating Maureen's Irish chili.

Here's Why: "Advise" is a verb, meaning the action of providing someone with counsel or suggestions on how she should behave. "Advice" is the noun meaning the suggestions themselves. You *advise* a person to do something. That something is the *advice* you offer. In this sentence, we're referring not to the action of offering a suggestion, but to the suggestion itself, namely that no more of this chili should be eaten. So the noun "advice" is right. Additional correct examples are:

Take my advice.
Problem students were advised by Mrs. Stanley.
As a first-year law student, Peter's legal advice wasn't all that trustworthy.

170

How dare you <u>advise</u> me to quit the same job you made me take!

84. Affect vs. Effect

> **Don't Say:** Larry was deeply *effected* by the new rule forbidding beef jerky on the job.
> **Say Instead:** Larry was deeply *affected* by the new rule forbidding beef jerky on the job.

Here's Why: The verb "affect" means to influence or to touch the feelings of someone, which is clearly what happened in this sentence with poor Larry. The verb "effect" is incorrect here because it means to bring something about, to cause something. "Effect" can also be a noun used to identify the result, the thing that has been brought about, as in *The effects of smoking are bad*. Here are some additional correct examples featuring "affect" and "effect":

Jane <u>effected</u> major design changes when she took over.

(Jane brought the changes about.)

Jane's new decor <u>affected</u> us all.

(The decor influenced or touched everyone.)

His stories <u>affect</u> me very deeply.

(They influence or touch me.)

The <u>effects</u> of this spending cut are unknown.

(Here "effects" is a noun, meaning the results.)

85. Amoral vs. Immoral

> **Don't Say:** Her *amoral* behavior was a bad influence on the children.
> **Say Instead:** Her *immoral* behavior was a bad influence on the children.

Here's Why: "Amoral" means to be completely outside the question of morality, neither good nor bad. "Immoral" means to be inside the boundaries, but to choose the wrong side. It means behavior that is not moral. In the example sentence, the meaning is that the mother's behavior is bad, so "immoral" is the word we want. Here are more correct examples:

Babies are <u>amoral</u> when they're born.

She thought her charitable donations compensated for her <u>immoral</u> acts.

Does Bobby's autism make him <u>amoral</u>, or does he understand the concepts of right and wrong?

He seems too kind to have done such an <u>immoral</u> thing.

86. Averse vs. Adverse

Don't Say: The pills made him green, but had no other *averse* effects.

Say Instead: The pills made him green, but had no other *adverse* effects.

Here's Why: "Averse" means to be in opposition. "Adverse" means unfavorable or bad. If it helps you, think of "bad" rhyming with the first syllable of "adverse." In this case, where we're talking about bad side effects, the word we want is "adverse." Additional correct examples are:

She was <u>averse</u> to all his opinions.

The pilot landed the plane under <u>adverse</u> conditions.

The court seems <u>averse</u> to that interpretation of the law.

He stopped writing after all the <u>adverse</u> criticism of his first book.

87. Beside vs. Besides

Don't Say: Hey, others *beside* you want to get through this checkout line.
Say Instead: Hey, others *besides* you want to get through this checkout line.

Here's Why: "Beside" without an "s" means to be at the side of. "Besides" with an "s" means in addition to, or moreover, as in our sentence here, where the idea is that others in addition to the person being rebuked would like to get through the line. Here are more correct examples:

He's smart and handsome and rich <u>besides</u>.
Well, I'll sit <u>beside</u> him, but I don't have to like it.
<u>Besides</u> Lynn, there will be four people going today.
Please put the sofa down <u>beside</u> the chair, or maybe <u>beside</u> the table, or wait—maybe <u>beside</u> the window.

88. Biannually vs. Biennially

Don't Say: The PTA elections were held *biannually*—in even numbered years.
Say Instead: The PTA elections were held *biennially*—in even numbered years.

Here's Why: This one's tricky: Both words begin with the prefix "bi-," which means two. But "biennially" means every two years, and "biannually" means twice a year. If it helps you, think of the "annual" in "biannually" as a reminder that you're talking about a single year's worth of time. Here are two other correct examples:

The <u>biannual</u> status report comes out each January and June.
Enjoy these blooms now—they're <u>biennials</u>, so they won't be here next spring.

89. Climatic vs. Climactic

> **Don't Say:** The *climactic* conditions made travel difficult.
> **Say Instead:** The *climatic* conditions made travel difficult.

Here's Why: "Climactic," which comes from "climax," refers to a dramatic event, a peak moment. "Climatic," which comes from "climate," refers, of course, to the prevailing weather conditions. That extra little "c" in there makes all the difference. Here are additional correct examples:

At the play's climactic moment, he yelled, "Don't open it!" to the actor on stage.

The problems with the trip to Antarctica weren't social, they were climatic.

The war was the climactic event in his presidency.

The farmers met to discuss climatic issues such as the drought.

90. Could of vs. Could have

> **Don't Say:** I *could of* danced all night.
> **Say Instead:** I *could have* danced all night.

Here's Why: This error springs from a common trick on the ear: The word "have" often sounds like the word "of" in everyday speech. So lots of the great helping verb teams in English—such as could *have*, would *have*, should *have*, may *have*, and might *have*—sound like could *of*, should *of*, and so on. This is especially true when "have" is contracted—when, for example, "should have" becomes "should've." But don't be fooled. You want to avoid two related errors here: In formal speech, avoid pronouncing "have" like "of," and when you're writing, make sure to use "have." Here are additional correct examples:

Bob <u>shouldn't have</u> ordered the Ultimate Texas Chili if he's recovering from an ulcer.

I <u>would have</u> let you drive if you'd asked me.

We <u>might have</u> lost our last opportunity to see a baseball game this season.

91. Elude vs. Allude

Don't Say: Did Sandy *elude* to her first marriage when you talked?

Say Instead: Did Sandy *allude* to her first marriage when you talked?

Here's Why: "Elude" and "allude" have very different meanings. "Elude" means to escape or avoid, as in *The thief eluded the police.* But "allude" means to refer to something indirectly, as in *He alluded to his ambitions, but wouldn't come right out and tell us what he wanted.* Two additional correct examples are:

I <u>eluded</u> discovery by changing my name to Guido.

Her poetry seems cheery, but it <u>alludes</u> to a troubled childhood.

92. Imminent vs. Eminent

Don't Say: After her graffiti episode at the office, Amy wondered if her dismissal were *eminent.*

Say Instead: After her graffiti episode at the office, Amy wondered if her dismissal were *imminent.*

Here's Why: "Eminent" is an adjective meaning famous or distinguished. "Imminent" describes a thing that is about to happen. In the example, Amy is wondering if she is about to be fired, so "imminent" is correct. Other correct examples are:

I don't care if he is an <u>eminent</u> psychologist; he eats with his fingers, and I won't invite him.

His palm reader said that a love affair was <u>imminent</u>.

Their unfortunate noses are the Brooks family's most <u>eminent</u> feature.

Disaster was <u>imminent</u> from the moment he lit the match to look for oil.

93. Ingenious vs. Ingenuous

Don't Say: They crafted an *ingenuous* plan for the takeover.
Say Instead: They crafted an *ingenious* plan for the takeover.

Here's Why: These words are virtual opposites. "Ingenuous" means artless or naïve. "Ingenious" means clever and resourceful, often with a dash of trickiness thrown in. The meaning of our sentence here is that these people have come up with a clever plan, not an artless one, so "ingenious" is the word we want. Additional correct examples are:

Her <u>ingenuous</u> remarks were unwelcome at the sophisticated dinner party.

Bill's <u>ingenious</u> invention won the top prize.

The insecure director avoided the <u>ingenuous</u> critic.

94. Jibe vs. Jive

Don't Say: These figures don't *jive*.
Say Instead: These figures don't *jibe*.

Here's Why: "Jibe" means to agree, to correspond. "Jive" refers to a kind of music or dance and also the slang term used to describe them, as in "jive talk." So here we need "jibe." Additional correct examples are:

He plays <u>jive</u> at a little club downtown.
The details of your story don't <u>jibe</u> with hers.

95. Tack vs. Tact

> **Don't Say:** The editor told Kim to take another *tact* with her story.
> **Say Instead:** The editor told Kim to take another *tack* with her story.

Here's Why: "Tact" means the quality of being adept at dealing with others, particularly where personal feelings are involved. This sentence isn't about that. "Tack" means a course of direction or policy; in this case, the angle Kim's story is taking. Here are more correct examples:

It took real <u>tact</u> to correct him without angering him.
Don't take that <u>tack</u> with Ann if you want your raise.
His lack of <u>tact</u> makes Mr. Stevens a terrible diplomat.
Don't give up; try another <u>tack</u> first.

96. Tortuous vs. Torturous

> **Don't Say:** That dental examination was *tortuous*.
> **Say Instead:** That dental examination was *torturous*.

Here's Why: What a difference a little "r" makes. "Tortuous" means winding, crooked, a complicated path, as in *The road across the mountains was tortuous*. "Torturous" means full of pain or torture, which is what this poor soul is saying about the visit to the dentist's. Here's another correct example of each:

His logic was so <u>tortuous</u> that none of us could follow it.
The test was <u>torturous</u> for those students who hadn't studied.

Test: Mixing up Words That Sound the Same

Please circle the correct choice.

1. She (accepted, excepted) his roses, but rejected his proposal.

2. Everyone (accept, except) Debbie had given the newly-weds a toaster.

3. My uncle never lets me leave without giving me plenty of financial (advice, advise).

4. I'd (advise, advice) you to stop using that expensive computer in the shower.

5. His whining and groveling had not the least (affect, effect) on my decision.

6. My decision was not the least (affected, effected) by his whining and groveling.

7. Carol Ann's dramatic new haircut has (affected, effected) a complete transformation in her personality.

8. It's illogical to get angry at an (amoral, immoral) force such as a tornado.

9. It may be as easy as taking candy from a baby, but it's also just as (amoral, immoral).

10. I've suffered few (averse, adverse) (affects, effects) from our 30-mile hike.

11. After Colin broke all the champagne glasses, we were (averse, adverse) to letting him wash the dishes again.

12. Jean-Paul hates to sit (beside, besides) anyone more handsome than he is.

13. I haven't told a soul (beside, besides) Ted—and Shelia, and Darryl, and Lucy.

14. Lorenzo has been married four times in the past eight years—his weddings are a (biannual, biennial) event.

15. Each spring and fall we do our (biannual, biennial) housecleaning.

16. The opera's (climactic, climatic) moment comes when the tenor jabs the mezzo-soprano with a salad fork.

17. The lecture told us a lot about global (climactic, climatic) patterns, but we still don't know if it will rain on Tuesday.

18. Fifi had successfully (eluded, alluded) her pursuers, but she was completely lost and hadn't eaten for hours.

19. After an hour of small talk, he finally (eluded, alluded) to his purpose in calling the meeting.

20. Harrison often boasted of his uncle, an (eminent, imminent) mountain climber.

21. When we heard the roar of a motorcycle, we knew his girlfriend's arrival was (eminent, imminent).

22. Nancy has invented an (ingenious, ingenuous) new car powered entirely by cholesterol.

23. The scheming villain easily extracted the secret from the (ingenious, ingenuous) child.

24. His testimony at the trial doesn't (jibe, jive) with what he said to reporters.

25. Lucinda, who is not well known for her (tact, tack), demanded to know why they had broken up.

26. When he proved deaf to all reasonable arguments, we tried a different (tact, tack) and called the police.

27. Biff's violin recital was a (tortuous, torturous) experience for lovers of good music.

28. She petrified us by driving down the (tortuous, torturous) cliff-side road at 70 miles an hour.

Answer Key: Mixing up Words That Sound the Same

1. accepted.
2. except.
3. advice.
4. advise.
5. effect.
6. affected.
7. effected.
8. amoral.

9. immoral.
10. adverse, effects.
11. averse.
12. beside.
13. besides.
14. biennial.
15. biannual.
16. climactic.
17. climatic.
18. eluded.
19. alluded.
20. eminent.
21. imminent.
22. ingenious.
23. ingenuous.
24. jibe.
25. tact.
26. tack.
27. torturous.
28. tortuous.

Mixing up Words That Look the Same

CHAPTER 9

In Chapter 8 we examined words that *sound* the same; in this unit, we'll learn to tell apart words that *look* the same—like members of the same family that all have the same peculiar nose. Some of these words are pretty common. Others are words we read more often than we hear, so when it comes time to use one, we often confuse it with one of its close cousins. But even though the words look alike, they can't do the same things in our sentences: just like two twins won't do the same things if one happens to be a plumber and the other happens to be a ballet dancer.

97. Adapt vs. Adopt

Don't Say: After one week with the kids, Quentin was already *adopting* to their behavior.
Say Instead: After one week with the kids, Quentin was already *adapting* to their behavior.

Here's Why: "To adapt" means to adjust to something or to make something suitable. "To adopt" means to accept or to take as one's own. In this sentence, we're talking about Quentin adjusting to the behavior of the children, not taking their behavior as his own—another possibility, and a humorous one, but not the intended meaning here. A few additional correct examples are:

> Melinda adapted quickly to her new job.
> The UN will adopt that resolution.
> We'll adapt the building to make it wheelchair accessible.

98. Allusion vs. Illusion vs. Delusion

> **Don't Say:** He made *illusions* to his book in every speech.
> **Say Instead:** He made *allusions* to his book in every speech.

Here's Why: With these three words, one little syllable makes all the difference. "Illusions" are false impressions. "Delusions" are closely related—they are also false impressions—but "delusion" also conveys a sense of being acted upon, as when a person's delusions of grandeur make her give up her day job. "Allusions" are completely different. They are indirect references to something, which is what's happening in the example sentence—the speaker makes indirect references to his book. So "allusions" is the right choice. Here's another correct example of each:

> The bridge looked as if it were swaying, but that was just an illusion right?
> Perry had harbored so many delusions about being promoted that he refused to believe he was fired.
> The Nine Lives Society loved the allusions to reincarnation in your poem.

99. Assignment vs. Assignation

> **Don't Say:** Lee's *assignation* was to finish the analysis by March.
> **Say Instead:** Lee's *assignment* was to finish the analysis by March.

Here's Why: Boy, you don't want to confuse these two nouns. "Assignation" means the act of making an assignment. But is also means a tryst or an arranged meeting, usually between two lovers. "Assignment" refers to the task itself that someone has given you to do. Now it's possible to have an assignation as your assignment if you are, say, a spy or something. But even then, the words aren't interchangeable. So here, where we're talking about a regular old project that Lee has been given to do, "assignment" is what we want. Additional correct examples are:

Your <u>assignment</u> is on the microfilm in your shoe.
Their <u>assignations</u> were brief and secret.
The <u>assignation</u> of Trevor to that post was shocking.
(We're talking about the action that someone had taken in assigning Trevor, not the assignment itself.)
Give me a more original excuse than "the dog ate my <u>assignment</u>."

100. Childlike vs. Childish

> **Don't Say:** Dr. Levin still has the same *childish* wonder about science that he had as a boy.
> **Say Instead:** Dr. Levin still has the same *childlike* wonder about science that he had as a boy.

Here's Why: "Childish" and "childlike" both describe the qualities of children, but they have very different meanings. "Childish" is a negative reference to children's lack of maturity, their silliness. "Childlike" is a positive reference to the innocence and unselfconsciousness of children. So in this sentence, where the intent is clearly to describe the doctor in positive terms, "childlike" is the appropriate choice. Additional correct examples are:

> Dana's <u>childish</u> behavior during poker games led to the breakup of the group.
> She has a <u>childlike</u> optimism about the future.
> He threw a <u>childish</u> tantrum when his dog took third place at the show.
> Mike bounced back from his trauma with a <u>childlike</u> resiliency.

101. Continual vs. Continuous

Don't Say: Tilly's phone rang *continuously* until her father disconnected it.
Say Instead: Tilly's phone rang *continually* until her father disconnected it.

Here's Why: There's a very subtle shade of difference here. "Continuously" refers to something that goes on without any interruption whatsoever. "Continually" refers to something that recurs at frequent intervals. In this case, the meaning is that many calls came in—at intervals that were too short for her father's liking. So "continually" is correct. Other correct examples are:

> Dave ran <u>continuously</u> for six hours, then collapsed.
> She claimed she made <u>continual</u> efforts to reach him.
> Gina's string of handball victories was <u>continuous</u>.
> For weeks, Don proposed to her <u>continually</u> until Shirley agreed to marry him.

184

102. Creditable vs. Credible vs. Credulous

Don't Say: We were surprised by the actor's *credulous* portrayal of a woman.
Say Instead: We were surprised by the actor's *credible* portrayal of a woman.

Here's Why: "Credulous" means to be gullible, ready to believe just about anything, as in *a credulous child*. "Credible" means to be worthy of belief, as in *a credible story*. And "creditable" means to be worthy of receiving credit or praise, as in *a creditable effort on a job*. In this case, where the meaning is that a man is playing a woman's part, the issue is one of believability, and so "credible" is the most appropriate choice. We could also have given the sentence a slightly different sense by saying that his performance was "creditable," meaning that it was worthy of praise. But "credulous," meaning gullible, just doesn't work. Here's another correct use of each:

He was too <u>credulous</u> to be trusted with the negotiations.
She did a <u>creditable</u> job on that assignment.
Sharon is the most <u>credible</u> speaker on the circuit.

103. Incredible vs. Incredulous

Don't Say: That excuse is simply *incredulous*.
Say Instead: That excuse is simply *incredible*.

Here's Why: These two words are the opposite numbers of "credible" and "credulous." "Incredible" means not credible or not believable, without credibility. It is often applied in a positive sense to things that are so good they're almost unbelievable—*his luck is incredible*—but the true sense of the word is "not believable." "Incredulous," on the other hand, means skeptical, unwilling to believe—the opposite of credulous, which means that someone is too ready to believe. In this

185

sentence, we're not talking about a person's being skeptical, we're talking about an excuse being unbelievable, so "incredible" is correct. Other correct examples are:

Julia's expression was <u>incredulous</u> during the speech on aliens from outer space.
I can see you are <u>incredulous</u>, but my story is true.
Sir, your accounts of your whereabouts on the evening of the ninth are <u>incredible</u>.
Phil's demonstrated <u>incredible</u> skill on the trampoline.

104. Elegy vs. Eulogy

Don't Say: The song was a *eulogy* mourning the death of his father.
Say Instead: The song was an *elegy* mourning the death of his father.

Here's Why: An "elegy" is a song or poem that mourns one who has died. A "eulogy" is a formal statement or speech expressing praise. Eulogies, of course, are often given at funerals, where the idea is to remember and praise the person who has died. But the word also applies to happier circumstances. One might, for instance, give a eulogy for an honored guest at a dinner. Here are additional correct examples:

The poet's musings on death resulted in his famous <u>elegy</u> for his father.
Dana didn't feel she had known Jim well enough to give the <u>eulogy</u> at the service.
The president delivered a <u>eulogy</u> to the heroes who came to the capitol.

105. Epitaph vs. Epithet

Don't Say: What was the *epithet* on her tombstone?
Say Instead: What was the *epitaph* on her tombstone?

186

Here's Why: An "epitaph" is an inscription on a tombstone in memory of the deceased. An "epithet" is a characterization, often negative, of a person. "Rosy-cheeked" and "slimeball" are epithets. Here are additional correct examples of each:

> Dan always liked the famous cowboy <u>epitaph</u> "he died with his boots on."
> The bully hurled <u>epithets</u> at the unattractive boy.
> I always wanted someone to use the <u>epithet</u> "lean and mean" to refer to me.

106. Flaunt vs. Flout

> **Don't Say:** The former 98-pound weakling *flouted* his new muscles on the beach.
> **Say Instead:** The former 98-pound weakling *flaunted* his new muscles on the beach.

Here's Why: "Flaunt" means to show off, which is what this guy was doing with his new physique. "Flout," on the other hand, means to go against and show contempt for tradition, rules, or authority, as in *James Dean played rebels who flouted tradition*. A few more correct examples are:

> She <u>flaunted</u> her wealth by wearing diamond-studded sneakers to the gym.
> The rules were <u>flouted</u> at every turn by the unruly kids.
> The party was a perfect chance for Julia to <u>flaunt</u> her cooking skills.
> Drew <u>flouts</u> convention by coloring his hair green.

107. Luxurious vs. Luxuriant

> **Don't Say:** They pitched tents, but Sheila went to a *luxuriant* hotel.
> **Say Instead:** They pitched tents, but Sheila went to a *luxurious* hotel.

Here's Why: "Luxuriant" means growing profusely. "Luxurious" means supplied with extreme comfort or luxury. So unless Sheila's hotel was growing profusely, "luxurious" is the word we want. Additional correct examples are:

> The jungle foliage was luxuriant.
> Ms. Amandson preferred a small house to the luxurious surroundings in which she'd been raised.
> She washed her luxuriant hair in a luxurious marble-tiled shower.

108. Morale vs. Moral

> **Don't Say:** Company *moral* went way up when they abandoned the dress code.
> **Say Instead:** Company *morale* went way up when they abandoned the dress code.

Here's Why: "Moral" is both an adjective and a noun. The adjective "moral" is used to describe something as either virtuous or as concerned somehow with good and bad, right and wrong. The noun "moral" means the lesson derived from a fable or event, as in *the moral of the story is....* The plural noun "morals" refers to the combined qualities that make a person virtuous, as in *Have you no morals?* or *He was a person of high income but low morals.* "Morale," on the other hand, is a noun referring to the state of mind, the attitude of a person or a group. In this sentence, we're clearly talking about the group's attitude improvement once suits and ties go by the wayside. Other correct examples are:

> His morale was high after the commander's speech.
> Do you think morale could be any lower around here?
> That woman has no morals.
> Theresa struggled to make a moral decision.

109. Periodic vs. Periodical

Don't Say: Wanting *periodical* updates on their affair doesn't make me a gossip.
Say Instead: Wanting *periodic* updates on their affair doesn't make me a gossip.

Here's Why: "Periodic" is an adjective referring to something that happens at regular intervals, such as periodic visits to the dentist. But "periodical" is a noun used only for publications, such as magazines, which appear at regular intervals. A few more examples of these including the related adverb "periodically" are:

You'll find that newsletter with the other periodicals.
Murphy told his boss that periodic trips to the French Riviera would be required for the project.
She stops in periodically when she's out of money.

110. Persecute vs. Prosecute

Don't Say: They should stop *prosecuting* them for their religious beliefs.
Say Instead: They should stop *persecuting* them for their religious beliefs.

Here's Why: "Prosecute" means to bring legal action against someone who is charged with a crime. "Persecute" means to harass someone for her beliefs or characteristics, which is why it's correct in this sentence. Other correct examples are:

After being persecuted for years, they formed their own political party.
I know you are guilty, and I hope they prosecute you to the fullest extent of the law.
He thinks they will persecute him for speaking out against the company's policy.

189

111. Proceed vs. Precede

> **Don't Say:** Stan, please get off the table so we can *precede* with the meeting.
>
> **Say Instead:** Stan, please get off the table so we can *proceed* with the meeting.

Here's Why: "Proceed" means to move forward. "Precede" means to come before something else." In this sentence, we're talking about getting on with the meeting, so "proceed" is the word we want. Additional correct examples are:

Darlene <u>preceded</u> Tom as president.
Shall we <u>proceed</u> with the dinner as planned?
Your act will <u>precede</u> the fire-eater's, so keep it short.
They have been instructed to <u>proceed</u> when ready.

112. Respectful vs. Respective

> **Don't Say:** How can I be *respective* of your wishes when you won't tell me what they are?
>
> **Say Instead:** How can I be *respectful* of your wishes when you won't tell me what they are?

Here's Why: "Respective" is a term of separation or comparison, as in *they went to their respective seats*, and *they were paid in accordance with their respective ranks*. "Respectful" means to be full of respect. So in this case, where respect for one's wishes is the issue, "respectful" is the appropriate choice. Additional correct examples are:

The cat kept a <u>respectful</u> distance from the Great Dane.
Go to your <u>respective</u> corners, then come out swinging.
The bears had a fall party and then went back to their <u>respective</u> caves for the winter.
Was your tone <u>respectful</u> when you demanded that overdue raise?

113. Sensuous vs. Sensual

Don't Say: She finds a *sensual* pleasure in classical music.
Say Instead: She finds a *sensuous* pleasure in classical music.

Here's Why: "Sensual" means pertaining to the senses, especially the sexual sense of senses. In 1641, John Milton made up the word "sensuous" in order to avoid the sexual connotations of "sensual" in one of his poems—and the word stuck. (Isn't English great?) These two words are very closely related, but the rule of thumb is that you use "sensuous" when you are referring to something giving pure aesthetic pleasure, and "sensual" when you wish to imply a more sexual meaning or to imply that the feeling involved is purely physical. Here are a few examples:

Let's go to the candy store, put on our bibs, and riot in <u>sensuous</u> pleasure.
Gilbert took a <u>sensuous</u> pleasure from the sight of a beautiful sunset.
Put down that <u>sensual</u> lingerie catalog this minute.
I don't think I'm ready to hear about your <u>sensual</u> side.

One word of warning on "sensual/sensuous": because the two words are so often confused, and because "sensual" very frequently has a sexual association, many people are likely to assume that you intend a sexual implication when you use either word. (This is a common, if unfortunate, process as a language changes: Whenever a word becomes associated with a sexual meaning, that meaning tends to become the dominant one.) If you want to be extra cautious, then, you might want to avoid "sensuous" altogether when you're talking about chocolate or music rather than a lingerie catalog.

114. Simple vs. Simplistic

> **Don't Say:** Don't overcomplicate this; we need a *simplistic* solution.
> **Say Instead:** Don't overcomplicate this; we need a *simple* solution.

Here's Why: You know what "simple" means: modest, uncomplicated, free of ornamentation. It's "simplistic" that throws people off. It's not just another word for simple—it's a negative term meaning something that has been oversimplified by ignoring complexity. Here in the example sentence, the speaker is looking for a simple answer, not one so oversimplified as to be unhelpful. Here are a few more examples:

> In Jim's <u>simplistic</u> view, everyone is either good or bad.
> They had a <u>simple</u> plan for rescuing the hostages.
> Her message is too <u>simplistic</u> to take seriously.

115. Uninterested vs. Disinterested

> **Don't Say:** I'm *disinterested* in hearing all the details of your uncle's ingrown toenail operation.
> **Say Instead:** I'm *uninterested* in hearing all the details of your uncle's ingrown toenail operation.

Here's Why: If you're "uninterested" in something, that means it doesn't interest you; it bores you. That's the meaning the sentence requires here. "Disinterested" means something quite different—that someone is impartial and unbiased: *Jill can't give you disinterested advice about Bob, since he owes her money and ran over her cat with his truck.* Here, Jill can't claim to be *disinterested* or impartial because she too obviously has good grounds to bear a grudge against Bob. Other correct examples are:

Fred's boss was <u>uninterested</u> in his lame excuses.
You can trust the judge to make the right decision;
she's completely <u>disinterested</u>.

Test: Mixing up Words That Look the Same

1. The symphony will be played as (adapted, adopted) for soprano kazoo.

2. Kathy's friends abandoned her when she (adapted, adopted) six orphaned baby skunks.

3. The professor's (allusions, delusions, illusions) to Shakespeare seemed inappropriate in a lecture about the life cycle of the newt.

4. Ralph suffers from the (allusion, delusion, illusion) that he is the reincarnation of King Tut, but in fact he is the reincarnation of Queen Nefertiti.

5. At the end of the act, the magician makes the entire audience disappear, but it's only an (allusion, illusion).

6. Sam complained that his parents made him work all night on his French (assignation, assignment).

7. Is she sneaking out for an (assignation, assignment) with her flamenco instructor, or just going to meet her accountant?

8. Even when Cindy has to shovel the sidewalk, she still has a (childlike, childish) love for snow.

9. The senator's (childish, childlike) sulking delighted the press but irritated voters.

10. During the eight-hour trip, the children (continually, continuously) asked how long it would take to get there.

11. The car alarm will ring for two hours (continually, continuously) unless someone turns it off.

12. Her story about being a secret agent cracking an international cheese-smuggling ring doesn't seem (creditable, credible, credulous) to me.

193

13. His (creditable, credible, credulous) work on the project got him promoted to assistant vice president.

14. Steve's (creditable, credible, credulous) nature made it easy to persuade him that he didn't have to pay any taxes this year.

15. We were so angry that we were (uninterested, disinterested) in hearing Fifi's lame excuses.

16. Umberto and Paul agreed to let an/a (uninterested, disinterested) person adjudicate their dispute over who made the best polenta.

17. Maurice's least famous poem is a 500-line (elegy, eulogy) on the death of his parakeet.

18. At a dinner in Frank's honor, it soon became clear that the woman appointed to deliver his (elegy, eulogy) didn't know he was still alive and listening in the audience.

19. She dismissed him from her office, shouting several unprintable (epitaphs, epithets) after him.

20. We wandered through the cemetery and read aloud the most interesting (epitaphs, epithets) we saw.

21. Lisette can't resist (flaunting, flouting) her new sports car in front of the neighbors.

22. We recklessly (flaunted, flouted) the rule against walking on the grass.

23. In the finale, Chip will perform the (incredible, incredulous) feat of juggling six live chickens.

24. She laughed (incredibly, incredulously) when Jim claimed the cookies had been stolen by gypsies.

25. Bill lives in a (luxurious, luxuriant) mansion with mink carpets in all 15 bathrooms.

26. Estelle longed to toss her (luxurious, luxuriant) blond curls, but she was a brunette with a crew cut.

27. The crew's (moral, morale) was sinking as fast as the ship.

28. The story's (moral, morale) was clear: never irritate a gorilla.

29. His (periodic, periodical) coffee breaks made the meeting last far into the night.

30. My neighbor subscribes to such a dull (periodic, periodical) that it's not worth the trouble of reading her mail.

31. Everyone in town knows Barbara stole my stamp collection, but the sheriff says there isn't enough evidence to (persecute, prosecute) her.

32. They have been (persecuting, prosecuting) him with veiled threats and vague insinuations.

33. After the guests have met the groom's family, they will (precede, proceed) to the onsite therapist so they can recover from the experience.

34. The woman who (proceeded, preceded) you in this job was adored by all who knew her.

35. After the quarrel, we each retreated to our (respectful, respective) rooms and slammed our (respectful, respective) doors.

36. Doreen's (respectful, respective) behavior to her uncle degenerated soon after he cut her out of his will.

37. She ran off with Juan and Umberto not to riot in (sensual, sensuous) pleasure, but as a spiritual quest.

38. At 5 in the morning I'm still too sleepy to take (sensual, sensuous) delight in a symphony—so turn off that stereo!

39. We've replaced our complicated regulations with one (simple, simplistic) rule.

40. I'm being audited by the IRS and my dog has just died; "just cheer up" is a (simple, simplistic) suggestion to make under the circumstances.

Answer Key: Mixing up Words That Look the Same

1. adapted.
2. adopted.
3. allusions.
4. delusion.
5. illusion.
6. assignment.

7. assignation.
8. childlike.
9. childish.
10. continually.
11. continuously.
12. credible.
13. creditable.
14. credulous.
15. uninterested.
16. disinterested.
17. elegy.
18. eulogy.
19. epithets.
20. epitaphs.
21. flaunting.
22. flouted.
23. incredible.
24. incredulously.
25. luxurious.
26. luxuriant.
27. morale.
28. moral.
29. periodic.
30. periodical.
31. prosecute.
32. persecuting.
33. proceed.
34. preceded.
35. respective, respective.
36. respectful.
37. sensual.
38. sensuous.
39. simple.
40. simplistic.

Mixing up Words Whose Meanings Are Related

CHAPTER 10

In Chapters 8 and 9 we covered usage problems that arise when we confuse two words because they sound or look the same. In this chapter, we'll take a look at words that are often mistaken for one another because their meanings are related in some way. These are almost always words we feel pretty comfortable with, which is why the trouble occurs—we aren't aware of, or we ignore, subtle differences in meaning. Though these nuances can seem bewildering, they give English its depth and exactitude in expression. And getting them right separates the men and women from the boys and girls when it comes to polished speaking.

116. Annoy vs. Irritate vs. Aggravate

Don't Say: Doesn't his sing-song voice *aggravate* you?
Say Instead: Doesn't his sing-song voice *irritate* you?

Here's Why: "Aggravate" can be a synonym for "irritate," but this is a less precise use of the word. "Aggravate" can do one job that "irritate" can't: Its core meaning is "to make worse," as in *aggravate the problem*. "Irritate" means to rouse to impatience or anger. It also means to cause inflammation of the skin, as in *the new lotion irritated the rash*. "Annoy" is somewhat milder. It means to cause slight irritation by troublesome behavior, and often carries with it the sense of repeated actions or attacks. Depending on the degree of frustration the speaker wishes to convey in the example sentence, she may choose either "annoy" or "irritate." But "irritate" is preferred to "aggravate" because we're not talking specifically about making something worse. More correct examples of each:

His habits <u>annoy</u> me, but I can live with them.

Her habits <u>irritate</u> me so much that I don't think I can live with them any more.

Joe's frequent tardiness <u>aggravated</u> his situation with his boss.

The mosquitoes <u>annoyed</u> Sheldon, so he spent much of the barbecue indoors.

Donna was <u>irritated</u> by the doctor's casual attitude.

Stop walking away; you're just <u>aggravating</u> the problem.

117. Burglary vs. Robbery

Don't Say: Officer, they must have committed the *robbery* when we were on vacation.

Say Instead: Officer, they must have committed the *burglary* when we were on vacation.

Here's Why: Burglars don't like to get up close and personal with their victims. "Burglary" refers solely to the act of entering a place with the idea of taking something that doesn't belong to you, and then, if you aren't caught, taking it. "Robbery," on the other hand, is taking something from someone by force. There's no sneaking around involved—unless maybe you're an unlucky burglar who gets caught in the act and resorts to force to get the job done. In the example sentence, where the bad guys did their dirty deed while the family was gone, it's clearly a case of burglary. Additional correct examples are:

After she was <u>robbed</u> at gunpoint, Mary hated going out alone at night.

I can't imagine how we were <u>burglarized</u> the day after Scam Security Systems came and installed our alarm.

The threat of highway <u>robbery</u> made a lot of carriage travelers nervous.

He took up <u>burglary</u> just so he could wear a black cat suit and climb up the side of buildings at night.

118. Can vs. May

> **Don't Say:** *Can* I use your lucky bowling ball?
> **Say Instead:** *May* I use your lucky bowling ball?

Here's Why: "Can" describes the ability to do something. "May" refers to the possibility that something may occur, and to the requesting or granting of permission. In this case, the speaker is clearly making a request, not asking if he is physically capable of using the ball. Other correct examples are:

You <u>may</u> go to the game if you promise not eat too many hot dogs like last time.

<u>Can</u> Mike finish building that popcorn statue before the wind kicks up?

Gee, you look lonely; <u>may</u> we join you?

<u>Can</u> you believe the report said it <u>may</u> snow tomorrow?

119. Compose vs. Comprise

> **Don't Say:** The club's athletic committee is *comprised* of 10 sedentary men.
> **Say Instead:** The club's athletic committee is *composed* of 10 sedentary men.

199

Here's Why: Both "compose" and "comprise" are about the relationship between parts and the whole. But the two words come at that relationship from different sides. "Compose" means to make up. It refers to the act of creating a whole by assembling a bunch of parts (think of composing a symphony note by note). "Comprise" means to take in or to contain. Its frame of reference is the whole and what parts may be contained inside. The traditional rule of thumb for usage is: The whole *comprises* the parts; the parts are *comprised in* the whole; the parts *compose* the whole; the whole is *composed of* the parts. In the example sentence, the meaning is that the 10 sedentary men, in this case, the parts, make up the whole, which in this case is the committee. Therefore, "composed of" is the correct choice. "Comprised of" is never correct. Here are more examples:

> The new congressional district <u>comprises</u> more ethnic groups than before.
> Eight players cannot <u>compose</u> a baseball team.
> The jury <u>comprise</u>d six men and six women.
> His argument was <u>composed</u> of weak points.
> His argument <u>comprised</u> weak points.

120. Convince vs. Persuade

Don't Say: How did you *convince* them to fly across the country for dinner?
Say Instead: How did you *persuade* them to fly across the country for dinner?

Here's Why: "Convince" means to succeed in getting someone to believe a statement or a proposition. "Persuade" also means bringing someone around to a particular way of thinking, but it carries the sense of persuading to action. If you can *convince* someone it's about to storm, chances are you can *persuade* him to stay inside. Additional correct examples are:

Please stop talking; your arguments <u>convinced</u> me an hour ago.

Steve <u>persuaded</u> his wife to run for the state senate.

How did he <u>convince</u> you that drinking all that beet juice was a good idea?

Were your teeth red after he <u>persuaded</u> you to drink all that beet juice?

121. Eager vs. Anxious

Don't Say: Leonard is *anxious* to meet Sylvia because he heard she plays a mean trombone.

Say Instead: Leonard is *eager* to meet Sylvia because he heard she plays a mean trombone.

Here's Why: "Anxious" means to be concerned, worried, full of anxiety. "Eager" means that you're looking forward to something with pleasure. So unless Leonard is going to be competing against Sylvia for the same trombone spot in a band, he's not anxious to meet her, but eager. Additional correct examples are:

Bradley was <u>anxious</u> about seeing his old girlfriend because he had gained so much weight.

The citizens were <u>anxious</u> about the president's ill health.

We are <u>eager</u> to settle this strike.

I'm <u>eager</u> to get to the honeymoon, because planning this wedding is wearing me out.

122. Explicit vs. Implicit

Don't Say: The warning was *implicit*: Do Not Open Near Fire!

Say Instead: The warning was *explicit*: Do Not Open Near Fire!

Here's Why: The world would be a dangerous place if warning labels were implicit. "Implicit" comes from "implied" and refers to something that is not said outright but that is understood. "Explicit" is something said outright, something made very clear. In this case, the warning label was obviously a clear, up-front expression, so "explicit" is the right choice. Additional correct examples are:

> How could you ignore the explicit instructions I gave you in my memo?
>
> Her eyes told the sad story implicitly.
>
> If you're not interested in seeing her again, you should state your feelings explicitly.
>
> The message implicit in his look was "go ahead and do it, just don't tell me the details."

123. Figuratively vs. Literally vs. Virtually

Don't Say: He was, *literally* speaking, up to his neck in paperwork.

Say Instead: He was, *figuratively* speaking, up to his neck in paperwork.

Here's Why: "Literally" means according to the literal meaning of the words—actually true. So unless this poor man is really, truly buried up to the neck in stacks of paper, "literally" is incorrect. "Figuratively" means according to or based on a figure of speech—metaphorical. And that's clearly the meaning of this sentence. "Virtually" means that for all practical purposes a thing is true, or that it is almost or nearly so, as in *virtually covered with dirt*. Here are correct examples of each:

> Once George put those suction cups on, he was literally climbing the walls.
>
> They called you the "hired gun" on this project, but I hope that's not literally true.

If you betray me, I'll tear you limb from limb—but of course, I mean that <u>figuratively</u>.

I am rich in a <u>figurative</u> sense because I have a full and happy life.

Shelly has read <u>virtually</u> the entire dictionary; for some reason, she just skipped the words beginning with *X*.

He waited until the talking had <u>virtually</u> stopped before addressing the group.

124. Imply vs. Infer

Don't Say: When you say, "get out," are you *inferring* that you want me to leave?

Say Instead: When you say, "get out," are you *implying* that you want me to leave?

Here's Why: The difference between "imply" and "infer" is in their points of view. Implying is something that's being done by the person (or thing) doing the communicating. His words or gestures are suggesting something beyond the literal meaning of his statements. Inferring, on the other hand, is done by the person on the receiving end of the communication. It's the action of reading between the lines to get at a meaning beyond the literal statement. In the example sentence, "implying" is correct, because the speaker is referring to the meaning suggested by the other's words, "get out." Here are some more correct examples—note that they include the noun forms of these verbs, "implication" and "inference":

His note <u>implied</u> that he would take action.

(The sentence is about the action of suggesting something, not about our action of reading between the lines.)

Laura <u>inferred</u> from that note that he would take action.

(Here the point of view is reversed—the sentence is about Laura's action of interpreting the note, not the note's act of communication.)

The <u>implications</u> of her speech on racism were frightening.

(The sentence is about what her speech communicated.)

We drew some frightening <u>inferences</u> from her speech on racism.

(The sentence is about what we took away from the speech, it's from our point of view.)

125. Kind of/Sort of vs. Rather

Don't Say: The evening was *kind of* boring, don't you think?
Say Instead: The evening was *rather* boring, don't you think?

Here's Why: Using "kind of" or "sort of" as substitutes for "rather" isn't the worst kind of usage infraction, but it is too informal for situations in which you want to be at your best. In those cases, use "kind of" or "sort of" to refer to a particular type or category, as in *What kind of dog is this?* And use "rather" as an alternative to "somewhat."

126. Let vs. Leave

Don't Say: I move that we *leave* the dress code stand.
Say Instead: I move that we *let* the dress code stand.

Here's Why: "Leave" means to depart and "let" means to allow. In this case, we're talking about allowing the dress code to stand, so "let" is correct. There is one circumstance in which "let" and "leave" are interchangeable, and that's when you're referring to someone not disturbing or interfering with something else—either "leave alone" or "let alone" is acceptable in those cases. Additional correct examples are:

<u>Let</u> him be, and he'll get over it.
Why don't you <u>leave</u> that to the experts?
If I agree to your terms, will you <u>let</u> the matter go?
I won't let you <u>leave</u> until you explain yourself!

127. Like vs. As/As If

> **Don't Say:** *Like* I said, pigs will fly before he calls.
> **Say Instead:** *As* I said, pigs will fly before he calls.

Here's Why: The word "like" has all sorts of meanings and appropriate uses. It can be a verb (I *like* him); a preposition (one thing is *like* another); an adjective (rainstorms and *like* weather problems); an adverb (worked *like* mad); and a noun (throw out hecklers and the *like*). But in standard English, "like" should not be used as a conjunction linking a complete clause ("I said") to the rest of the sentence. If you're making a comparison and all you want to do is link a lonely little noun to the rest of the sentence, you can use "like" in its capacity as a preposition: *she looks just like you* is correct. But if you want to link a complete clause, with a subject and verb, you need "as" or "as if": *The elections did not turn out as we hoped they would*. Here are some more sample sentences in which an incorrect "like" is changed to the correct "as" or "as if":

> *Instead of* Will you be here at 6 like you said you would? *say* Will you be here at 6 as you said you would?
> *Instead of* It took courage to fight like he did, *say* It took courage to fight as he did.
> *Instead of* She looks like she's going to win, *say* She looks as if she's going to win.
> *Instead of* You act like you're in charge, *say* You act as if you were in charge.

128. Likely vs. Apt vs. Liable

> **Don't Say:** I'm *liable* to show up for dinner any day of the week.
> **Say Instead:** I'm *likely* to show up for dinner any day of the week.

205

Here's Why: All three of these words are meant to suggest that a given thing is likely to happen. The distinctions among them are based on the situations and attitudes of the speaker and the thing she's speaking about. For example, "liable" should be used when the person you're talking about would be negatively affected by the outcome as in *she's liable to fall on that ice*. "Apt" is best used when the person or thing you're talking about is by its very nature making an outcome probable, and when the speaker is worried about that outcome, as in *that mad dog is apt to bite me*. "Likely" is the word you reach for when you just want to say something is likely to happen without conveying anything special about the subject of your sentence or your own concerns. Here are additional correct examples of each:

> You're liable to fall if you try to climb that rock without any training.
> When we saw her test scores, we knew she was liable to do poorly in school.
> Our short-tempered friend is apt to explode when he hears the news.
> That old car of yours is apt to leave you stranded on the highway someday.
> Marissa is likely to win the school's top honors.
> The plane is not likely to leave on time.

129. Percent vs. Percentage

Don't Say: What *percent* of the gross are you getting on that deal?
Say Instead: What *percentage* of the gross are you getting on that deal?

Here's Why: The rule for this one is easy. "Percent" can appear only after a number: *Twenty-five percent of all toddlers believe in the Easter Bunny*. "Percentage" doesn't like

206

to be that specific: It never appears in the company of a number, and it means a proportion or part of a whole. One thing to keep in mind about "percentage" is that it doesn't necessarily mean a *small* part of the whole, so you'll need an adjective to tell people how big the percentage is: *A large percentage of the audience walked out in indignation, but a small percentage thought the joke was funny and stayed to hear more.* Other correct examples are:

> She is taking a <u>percentage</u> of the profits and buying a year's worth of pickled herring.
> Only 5 <u>percent</u> of the students voted to ban jeans.
> Only a small <u>percentage</u> of people agreed with the verdict.
> His contract nets him a 2 <u>percent</u> royalty.

130. Quote vs. Quotation

> **Don't Say:** Jules filled his essay with inspirational *quotes* from his favorite author.
> **Say Instead:** Jules filled his essay with inspirational *quotations* from his favorite author.

Here's Why: While "quote" is very frequently used as a noun by the majority of educated speakers, some conservative speakers argue that "quote" is a verb and only a verb: *Can I quote you on that?* In very formal speech and writing, use "quotation" when you need a noun: *His quotations from the great philosophers were interesting, but had nothing to do with the subject at hand.*

131. Semiannually vs. Semimonthly vs. Semiweekly

> **Don't Say:** When I read the *semiweekly* newsletter on the first, I couldn't wait to see the next issue on the 15th.
> **Say Instead:** When I read the *semimonthly* newsletter on the first, I couldn't wait to see the next issue on the 15th.

Here's Why: The prefix "semi-" means "half. So "semi-weekly" means every half week, "semimonthly" means every half month, and "semiannually" means every half year. These terms are close cousins to the terms "biweekly," "bimonthly," and "biannually." But they go one step further to indicate the precise interval at which the event occurs, that is, by halves of whatever unit of time to which it is referring.

132. Serve vs. Service

> **Don't Say:** After the ceremony, the waiters will *service* the guests in their rooms.
>
> **Say Instead:** After the ceremony, the waiters will *serve* the guests in their rooms.

Here's Why: Whenever you're talking about *people* being served something, use "serve" as a verb and "service" as a noun: *The waiters serve the guests,* but *The waiters provide service to the guests.* If you're afraid *the waiters serve the guests* sounds as if the waiters are setting up a banquet for cannibals, then say what the waiters are serving the guests: *the waiters will serve the guests cucumber sandwiches in their rooms.*

Why avoid service as a verb? Well, there are two accepted meanings of "service" as a verb, and neither one is the sort of thing that waiters should be doing to guests. "Service" can correctly refer to work done on a machine: *The mechanic serviced my car* or *The repairman is servicing the washing machine.* Or—and this is why you REALLY need to be careful with "service"—it's a term in animal breeding for something that a very successful racehorse gets to do to a lot of mares after he retires, and no, we're not going to give you a sample sentence. But you can see the problem with saying that waiters in a reputable hotel service the guests, unless all that the guests are going to get is a nice cucumber sandwich.

133. Take vs. Bring

> **Don't Say:** Will you *bring* your books to the library when you go?
> **Say Instead:** Will you *take* your books to the library when you go?

Here's Why: The choice between "take" or "bring" is based on the point of view. If you wish to convey that something is being carried toward a place the speaker is speaking from or toward a place from which he would like the action to be considered, then use "bring." If the meaning is that the thing is being carried away from the speaker or from some particular place, then "take" is what you want. In this case, the point of view is that of the speaker and the listener—their current locations. He's talking about carrying the books away from there to the library, and that makes "take" the correct choice. If, on the other hand, this person got a call from the librarian, she would say *bring the books* because she is talking from the point of view of her location at the library, and the books are someplace else. Other correct examples are:

Why did you bring home the lunch I made you without eating it?
Are you taking Mimi to the Jacksons' dinner next Thursday?
The instructions said to bring a map.
He'll take everything with him when he leaves, except his toothbrush, which he always forgets.

134. Use vs. Utilize

> **Don't Say:** Mark *utilized* all his skills in the kitchen to boil water.
> **Say Instead:** Mark *used* all his skills in the kitchen to boil water.

Here's Why: "Use" is always correct; you can never go wrong if you use it exclusively and never use "utilize" at all. "Utilize" began life as pretentious jargon, and you'll still find some conservative speakers who think of it as just that. But other speakers argue that "utilize" expresses an important shade of meaning if it refers to putting something to *good* use, as opposed to wasting it or using it for an inappropriate purpose. In that sense it goes a step beyond the simple idea of using a thing. Still, "utilize" is too often employed when a simple "use" will do, as in the example sentence, and the result is a loss of clarity and an increase in pretentiousness. The only time you want to reach for "utilize" instead of "use" is when you are trying to make the distinction between the two. For example, *I couldn't utilize the diagrams* means that they couldn't be put to some good use, whereas *I couldn't use the diagrams* might be taken to mean that the speaker was incapable of using them. Additional correct examples are:

> I used the funds before I knew where they came from.
> They used every trick in the book to snare that client.
> It's a shame that none of those abandoned buildings can be utilized for the recreation program.

Test: Words Whose Meanings Are Related

Please circle the correct choice.

1. Dexter's arthritis was (annoyed, irritated, aggravated) when he insisted on performing in a trapeze act.
2. Although her continual requests for more sugar (annoyed, irritated, aggravated) me, I complied with them politely.
3. She was so (annoyed, irritated, aggravated) by his demands for money that she moved to another state.
4. (Can, May) I offer you another slice of pie?
5. (Can, May) you wiggle your ears?

6. If you promise to clean your room, you (may, can) go to the monster truck rally.

7. Kathy is so talented that she (can, may) balance her checkbook and sort her laundry at the same time.

8. The chili was (composed, comprised) of six ingredients, all spicy.

9. His dissertation on the meaning of the universe (composed, comprised) arguments he learned at his mother's knee.

10. Rex was (eager, anxious) about going to the dentist and (eager, anxious) to return home as soon as possible.

11. The alderman cheerfully claimed to be (eager, anxious) to cooperate with the investigation, but he looked pretty (eager, anxious) to me.

12. I posted a sign in the bathroom that (explicitly, implicitly) told him never, under any circumstances, to use my toothbrush, but he just ignored it.

13. When Barbara avoided him for a week, Theodore took it as an (implicit, explicit) signal that she wasn't going to repay the money.

14. I'm (figuratively, virtually) certain that your father won't let you borrow his new Porsche.

15. Juan was, (figuratively, literally) speaking, the hottest thing since nuclear fission.

16. Annette often claimed she ate like a bird, but when she ate that worm on a dare it became (figuratively, literally) true.

17. What am I to (imply, infer) from the presence of this lipstick on your collar?

18. The (implications, inferences) of Darlene's admiring glances and longing sighs terrified Lucius.

19. If you lock Egore in the basement when you go, you'll (imply, infer) you don't trust him alone with the baby.

20. We (implied, inferred) from Lauren's shifty eyes that she was indeed the culprit.

211

21. Billy felt (kind of, sort of, rather) sick when he saw the bug scuttling across his poached egg.

22. (Let, Leave) him sulk—we'll just ignore him.

23. If Greta says she wants to be alone, we'll (let, leave) her alone.

24. I refuse to date anyone who looks (like, as, as if) a frog.

25. I refuse to date anyone who looks (like, as, as if) he's just swallowed frog.

26. (Like, As, As if) I said, every silver lining has its cloud.

27. You're (likely, apt, liable) to have a bad accident if you don't pack your parachute more carefully.

28. Don't give a puppy to the mad scientist—he's (likely, apt, liable) to do something unpleasant with it.

29. Doreen is (likely, apt, liable) to be happy when she finally gets out of prison.

30. Miriam won't be president for long if a large (percent, percentage) of the club's members think she's incompetent.

31. A fraction of 1 (percent, percentage) of the profits go to charity.

32. The speech was enlivened by frequent (quotes, quotations) in ancient Greek.

33. We indulge in our semiweekly shopping spree (each Tuesday and Friday, on the first and 15th of each month).

34. Since you gave me your semimonthly lecture on the virtues of broccoli on March 1, I'm not due for another until (March 15, May 1).

35. Our department's semiannual audit happens (each spring and fall, in even-numbered years.)

36. The bellboys are on call 24 hours a day to (serve, service) the guests.

37. That restaurant has terrible food but wonderful (serve, service).

38. Leave me if you want, but be sure to (take, bring) that spoiled dog with you.

39. I asked him to (take, bring) seltzer water to my dinner party, but he (taken, brought) peanut butter instead.

40. Dahlia was trying to (use, utilize) a toothpick to pry open the lid.

41. Why are we (using, utilizing) all these index cards to keep track of the data when we could (use, utilize) the $5,000 computer that is currently being (used, utilized) as a very expensive coat rack?

Answer Key: Words Whose Meanings Are Related

1. aggravated.
2. annoyed.
3. irritated.
4. May.
5. Can.
6. may.
7. can.
8. composed.
9. comprised.
10. anxious, eager.
11. eager, anxious.
12. explicitly.
13. implicit.
14. virtually.
15. figuratively.
16. literally.
17. infer.
18. implications.
19. imply.
20. inferred.

21. rather. Use either "kind of" or "sort of" when you want to distinguish one type or class of thing from another: *What kind of* or *sort of bug is that scuttling across your poached egg?*

22. Let.

23. let *or* leave. Either is correct.

24. like.

25. as if.

26. As.

213

27. liable. It emphasizes that the speaker thinks the outcome would be bad; "likely" may also be used to express a simple probability.

28. apt. It emphasizes that the speaker thinks the outcome would be unpleasant, as well as something that a mad scientist might do out of his or her very nature. "Likely" may also be used to express a simple probability.

29. likely. It is the best choice here; the outcome isn't something unpleasant (which would make "liable" appropriate), and it's not something that Doreen's very nature makes her likely to do (which would make "apt" an appropriate choice).

30. percentage.

31. percent.

32. quotations.

33. each Tuesday and Thursday.

34. March 15.

35. each spring and fall.

36. serve.

37. service.

38. take.

39. bring, brought.

40. use.

41. using, utilize, used. Some very conservative speakers believe that "utilizes" is always pretentious and unnecessary. Others believe "utilizes" can express the idea of using sophisticated or rare resources in the best possible way. Here, the sentence distinguishes between "using" resources badly (using index cards to keep track of complex data, using a computer as a coat rack) and" utilizing" resources particularly well or efficiently (utilizing an expensive computer to track data).

Made-up Words

CHAPTER 11

People are always making up words. Usually the idea is to transform a noun or an adjective into a verb, say, for example, by turning the adjective "final" into the ersatz verb "finalize." And standards often evolve over time to accommodate these changes as the new words fall into widespread usage. But not all of these creations become acceptable, and those that do tend to take a long while—sometimes centuries—to get there. The thing you want to avoid is being ahead of the trend because instead of being perceived as a language maverick, you're more likely to be thought of as unrefined or pretentious. The following errors are the most common when dealing with made-up words.

135. Irregardless

Don't Say: We'll have the meeting *irregardless* of whether Stuart can attend.
Say Instead: We'll have the meeting *regardless* of whether Stuart can attend.

Here's Why: "Irregardless" is not a word. Somewhere along the line, somebody who didn't understand what "regardless" meant thought that the negative prefix "ir-" would make the word mean "without regard," the way you'd turn "relevant" into "irrelevant." But "regardless" already means "without regard"—that's the whole reason that "-less" suffix is tacked on to the back end in the first place. Using "irregardless" is a big signal that a speaker is uninformed. Don't do it.

136. Authored

> **Don't Say:** The Senator has *authored* a new recipe book devoted to cooking and eating crow.
> **Say Instead:** The Senator has *written* (or *published*) a new recipe book devoted to cooking and eating crow.

Here's Why: "Author" is a noun that identifies the *person* who did the writing—it should not be used as a verb describing the *action* of writing.

137. Critiqued

> **Don't Say:** Did you hear how Lisa *critiqued* Maureen's performance?
> **Say Instead:** Did you hear how Lisa *criticized* (or *reviewed*) Maureen's performance?

Here's Why: This is the same problem we had with "authored." "Critique" is a noun that shouldn't be turned into a verb. One explanation for why this happens is that the verb "criticize," which by definition carries neither positive nor negative connotations, has come to have a negative sense to it—so people turn to "critique" as an alternative. Avoid this.

138. Gift

> **Don't Say:** They *gifted* the university with a million-dollar donation.
> **Say Instead:** They *presented* the university with a million-dollar donation.

Here's Why: Again, "gift" is a noun that shouldn't be turned into a verb. There are obviously a lot of other ways this sentence could have been corrected, including *They made a million-dollar donation to the university* and *They gave a million dollars to the university.*

139. Adding "-ize"

> **Don't Say:** Every time Malcom's mail is late he says they should *privatize* the postal service.
>
> **Say Instead:** Every time Malcom's mail is late he says they should turn over the postal service to the *private* sector.

Here's Why: There are a lot of respectable "-ize" verbs such as "hospitalize," "jeopardize," and "institutionalize" that had to travel a long and rocky path to acceptability. But there are a number of "-ize" words in popular use—especially in business environments—that haven't made it yet into the halls of standard English. These include "privatize" from our example, as well as "finalize," "prioritize," "incentivize," and "theorize." These words sound like needless jargon at best and pretentious jargon at worst—they're best avoided by careful speakers and writers.

140. Enthuse

> **Don't Say:** The company president *enthused* over the new budget report until he discovered that it contained five mathematical errors.
>
> **Say Instead:** The company president *praised* (or *applauded*) the new budget report until he discovered that it contained five mathematical errors.

Here's Why: The verb "enthuse" is a fine word that performs a useful function: it conveys either the causing or the expressing of enthusiasm. But it's a relatively recent creation, and some conservative speakers still object to it. So enthuse away in ordinary conversation at home and at work; but in the most formal kind of speech and writing, however, you may wish to cater to the conservatives and avoid it.

141. Adding "-wise"

Don't Say: It's an interesting job, but not much *salary-wise*.
Say Instead: It's an interesting job, but the *salary is small*.

Here's Why: Lots of respectable words end in "-wise" as a way of indicating a manner or a direction—"clockwise" is a common example. However, tacking on the suffix "-wise" willy-nilly in order to convey "with regard to" is a no-no. Stay away from formulations such as "profit-wise," "time-wise," and "height-wise."

Test: Made-up Words

Please rewrite the following sentences, substituting preferred words for the words in italics. The Answer Key offers possible revisions; in many cases there's more than one way to revise.

1. My husband hated the vase, but I bought it *irregardless*.
2. That plant will die *irregardless* of whether you water it.
3. Earl has authored more than 80 books, including the best-selling *Tofu Fantasies*.
4. Warren *critiqued* every aspect of the concert, from the oboist's delightful solo to the conductor's terrible comb-over.
5. Aunt Hortense *gifted* the museum with her unparalleled collection of brass knuckles.
6. We flew to Tahiti to *finalize* the deal in more comfortable surroundings.
7. Mornings work best when you *prioritize* carefully: socks first, shoes afterward.
8. How can we *theorize* this contradiction?

218

9. She *enthused* about the opera at dinner, but immediately fell asleep when it began.

10. He's intelligent and charming, but *height-wise* he falls a little short.

11. We're doing fine *profit-wise*, but not too well *morale-wise*.

12. *Taste-wise* our product is way ahead of its competitors.

Answer Key: Made-up Words

1. My husband hated the vase, but I bought it <u>regardless</u>. *Or:* My husband hated the vase, but I bought it <u>anyway</u>.

2. That plant will die <u>regardless</u> of whether you water it. *Or:* That plant will die whether you water it or not.

3. Earl has <u>written</u> *or* <u>published</u> *or (more creatively)* <u>spawned</u> *or* <u>vomited</u> more than 80 books, including the best-selling *Tofu Fantasies*.

4. Warren <u>criticized</u> *or* <u>reviewed</u> *or* <u>considered</u> *or* <u>examined</u> *or* <u>discussed</u> every aspect of the concert, from the oboist's delightful solo to the conductor's terrible comb-over.

5. Aunt Hortense <u>gave</u> the museum her unparalleled collection of brass knuckles.

6. "Finalize" is pretty widely accepted; but you may wish to use the following revisions if you want to avoid language that sounds like "jargon": We flew to Tahiti to <u>complete</u> *or* <u>conclude</u> the deal in more comfortable surroundings.

7. Mornings work best when you <u>plan</u> carefully.

8. How can we <u>explain</u> *or* <u>discuss</u> *or* <u>account</u> for this contradiction? "Theorize" is pretty widely accepted as an intransitive verb that doesn't take an object, as in "Don't just theorize, get some practical experience!" But most speakers don't accept "theorize" as a transitive verb: if you need to have a direct object, choose an alternative to "theorize." Please note that not all "-ize" words are considered out-of-bounds. Unfortunately, there is no rule to tell you which are

219

correct: some "-ize" words have been around long enough to be accepted, while some have not. The following examples are probably the safest and most widely accepted: "She laughed so hard at his proposal that she had to be <u>hospitalized</u>." "Will this typhoon <u>jeopardize</u> our vacation plans?"

9. She <u>praised</u> the opera at dinner, but immediately fell asleep when it began.

10. He's intelligent and charming, but he's a little too short.

11. <u>We're making a lot of money.</u>

   Or: <u>Profits are up</u>, but morale is low.

12. Our product <u>tastes better</u> than its competitors.

Wasteful Words and Infelicities

CHAPTER 12

Speaking errors aren't always a matter of leaving out a word or using a word in the wrong way. Some errors result from too many words—such as the kind of murky or incorrect sentences you end up with when you sprinkle around an extra "a," "on," or "as" or two. The following sections include the most problematic errors that arise from tossing in an extra word where it doesn't belong:

142. A half a

Don't Say: Jerald ate *a half a* rhubarb pie before we could stop him.
Say Instead: Jerald ate *half a* rhubarb pie before we could stop him.

Here's Why: The first "a" here is unnecessary. Say either, *He ate one half of a pie*, or *He ate half of a pie*.

143. And et cetera

Don't Say: We took everything to the game—the blankets, the thermos, the stadium cushions, *and et cetera*.
Say Instead: We took everything to the game—the blankets, the thermos, the stadium cushions, *et cetera*.

Here's Why: The Latin phrase "et cetera" means "and other things." So putting an "and" in front of the phrase is unnecessary. Just say "et cetera" and be done with it.

144. Like

> **Don't Say:** Do you want to go for, *like*, a big dinner or just a snack?
> **Say Instead:** Do you want to go for a big dinner or just a snack?

Here's Why: The use of "like" in this way, just sprinkled in, is a big indicator of unpolished, informal speaking. It's a hard habit to break, but one worth working on, because a few of these "likes" in a sentence send all the wrong signals.

145. The field of

> **Don't Say:** What makes Susan interested in *the field of* engineering?
> **Say Instead:** What makes Susan interested in engineering?

Here's Why: "In the field of" is just a little more than you need to get the idea across here. It's not that there's anything grammatically wrong with the phrase, but it's clutter. You don't need it unless your whole meaning is about the field as a field, say, for example, if it were the subject of the sentence *The field of engineering is crowded.*

146. Needless to say

> **Don't Say:** *Needless to say*, this has been an exciting party.
> **Say Instead:** This has been an exciting party.

Here's Why: "Needless to say" can be an extremely useful expression, with either a serious or ironic meaning. As a serious expression, it can signal that you and your audience share a belief that's been challenged or threatened in some way: *He asked me to run away with him to Tahiti, but I refused, needless to say.* As an ironic expression, it can humorously flag an idea that you and your audience know is not true: *Needless to say, Grandma's been arrested five times for rioting and being disorderly in the streets.* In both of these legitimate uses of the phrase, it's meant to emphasize some important common assumptions you share with the people listening to you or reading your words: It creates a sense of community. But the phrase is often overused, as in our example, where it emphasizes an unimportant opinion—that a party has been exciting—rather than a crucial belief—that one shouldn't run off to Tahiti when one has other commitments, or that one's grandmother is a perfectly moral person. In this sort of case, "needless to say" is needless to say: It's clutter, and it can become a bad habit if you use it too often. Whenever you feel tempted to say "needless to say," ask yourself whether it's doing any meaningful work for you. If not, leave it out; save it for more important occasions.

147. Time period

> **Don't Say:** Alphonse and Mario had not seen each other for a very long *time period*.
> **Say Instead:** Alphonse and Mario had not seen each other for a very long *time*.

Here's Why: The word "period" carries with it a sense of time, so it's rare that you need to use both words together. Simply say *a long time* or *a designated period*.

148. Party

> **Don't Say:** Officer, she is the *party* who hit my car.
> **Say Instead:** Officer, she is the *one* who hit my car.

Here's Why: So who are you, a would-be district attorney? "Party" shouldn't be used as a substitute for "person" unless you're a lawyer writing a legal brief or a restaurant hostess, asking, *Are you with the Cooper party?* "Party" seems to get used in this way when someone believes a touch of formality is in order. But it's not only incorrect in this context, it's a sign that you're trying too hard. Even the district attorney, if he knows his stuff, would simply say *she's the one* or *she's the person* or even *she's the nut*—but never *she's the party*.

Test: Wasteful Words

Please revise the following sentences, replacing or eliminating the clutter words and phrases in italics.

1. When Melvyn sued Sarah for custody of their pet iguana, I was asked to adjudicate between the *two parties*.
2. He'd gulped down *a half a* glass of grape juice before he realized it was cough medicine.
3. One can find almost anything on his kitchen floor: dirty laundry, cans of cat food, the lost ark of the covenant, *and et cetera*.
4. I'm, *like*, so thrilled to, *like*, meet you that I can, *like*, barely speak.
5. Her parents wanted her to study *the field of* architecture, but Pauline was more interested in going to art school.
6. *Needless to say*, Stuart was wearing a pretty appalling tie this morning.
7. Vladimir has been waiting for Godot for a long *time period*.

Answer Key: Wasteful Words

1. When Melvyn sued Sarah for custody of their pet iguana, I was asked to adjudicate between the two of them.
2. He'd gulped down half a glass of grape juice before he realized it was cough medicine.
3. One can find almost anything on his kitchen floor: the lost ark of the covenant, et cetera.

   Make sure you pronounce "et cetera" correctly: not as "ex cetera," but with a hard "t" sound in the "et": "eT cetera."
4. I'm so thrilled to meet you that I can barely speak.
5. Her parents wanted her to study architecture, but Pauline was more interested in going to art school.

Again, "in the field of" isn't so much incorrect as unnecessary.

6. Stuart was wearing a pretty appalling tie this morning.

In this instance, "needless to say" belongs to the club of unnecessary phrases; it's not incorrect, just fluff.

7. Vladimir has been waiting for Godot for a long time.

Mispronounced Words

CHAPTER 13

Nothing brands your speaking as "unpolished" faster than mispronouncing words, particularly if they're common words. In this chapter, we'll help you with some of the most common pronunciation problems. There's no written test at the end of this unit, because a written test can't tell you much about how well you're pronouncing a word. Use the time you would have used quizzing yourself to practice saying these words out loud until the correct pronunciations feel more natural to you.

149. Air vs. Err

Don't Say: Air.
Say Instead: Err (rhymes with "purr").

Say "err" when you mean the verb "err," meaning to make an error, as in the phrase *to err is human.*

150. Anyways vs. Anyway

Don't Say: Anyways.
Say Instead: Anyway.

"Anyway" never, ever has an "s" at the end.

151. A ways vs. A way

Don't Say: A ways.
Say Instead: A way.

"Way" never has an "s" on the end when it's being used as part of the expression "a way," as in *she has a way to go*.

152. Cent vs. Cents

Don't Say: Five cent.
Say Instead: Five centS.

"Five cent" is perfectly fine as an adjective: *a five-cent gumball*. But when you use it as a noun, you need to add an "s" to "cent" if you're talking about more than one: *She can remember when stamps cost five cents. My parents gave me 25 cents when I lost a tooth, but I have to give my kids a dollar*. Compare these sentences to: *That 99-cent pen will break in three days*.

153. Libary vs. Library

Don't Say: Li-ba-ry.
Say Instead: Li-bRa-ry.

Make sure you pronounce both "r"s. "Li-bra-ry."

154. Reconize vs. Recognize

Don't Say: Re-<u>con</u>-ize.
Say Instead: Re-<u>coG</u>-nize.

Don't leave out the "g." It's "re-cog-nize."

155. Stricly vs. Strictly

Don't Say: Stri<u>c</u>-ly.
Say Instead: Stric<u>T</u>-ly.

Don't leave out the second "t." It's "strict-ly."

156. Heighth vs. Height

Don't Say: Heigh<u>th</u>.
Say Instead: Height (rhymes with "bite").

Perhaps people mispronounce "height" as "heighth" because they're thinking of the "th" at the end of "width." But it's wrong; "height" always ends with a simple "t."

157. Athaletics vs. Athletics

Don't Say: Ath-<u>a</u>-le-tics.
Say Instead: Ath-<u>le</u>-tics (just three syllables).

Leave out the extra "a." And this goes for the person, too. It's never "ath-a-lete," it's always "ath-lete."

158. Goverment vs. Government

Don't Say: Go-<u>ver</u>-ment.
Say Instead: Go-<u>verN</u>-ment.

Don't forget the first "n"—think of the verb, "gover<u>n</u>." "Go-ver<u>n</u>-ment."

159. Irrevelant vs. Irrelevant

Don't Say: Ir-<u>rev</u>-e-lant.
Say Instead: Ir-<u>RELL</u>-e-Vant.

Don't transpose the "l" and the "v." Think of the "rel" in the words "<u>rel</u>evant" and "<u>rel</u>ated." "Ir-<u>rel</u>-e-vant."

160. Temperment vs. Temperament

Don't Say: Tem-per-ment.
Say Instead: Tem-per-a-ment (say all four syllables).

There's a little "a" you have to sneak in near before the "ment." "Tem-per-a-ment."

161. Lightening vs. Lightning

Don't Say: Ligh-<u>ten</u>-ing.
Say Instead: Light-<u>ning</u> (two syllables).

Say "lightning" when you're referring to the thing that happens during a storm. "Light<u>ening</u>" (three syllables) means that something is becoming lighter.

162. Mischevious vs. Mischievous

Don't Say: Mis-che-<u>vi</u>-ous.
Say Instead: Mis-chie-<u>vous</u> (three syllables, mis-cha-vuss).

"Mische<u>vi</u>ous" is not a word. Leave out the extra "ee" sound. It's always "mis-chie-<u>vous</u>."

163. Grevious vs. Grievous

Don't Say: Gre-<u>vi</u>-ous.
Say Instead: Grie-<u>vous</u> (two syllables, gree-vuss).

Like "mischievous," "grievous" is a word people love to stick an extra "ee" sound into—but it's always "grievous."

164. Histry vs. History

> **Don't Say:** His-try.
> **Say Instead:** His-tor-y (three syllables).

Only an Englishman gets to say "his-try." You need "tor," in there when you're in America, my friend. "His-tor-y."

165. Nucular vs. Nuclear

> **Don't Say:** Nu-cu-lar.
> **Say Instead:** Nuc-le-ar (nu-CLEE-ar).

The word comes from "nucleus." So you must begin "nuclear" the same way, with "nu-clee," never "nu-cue." It's "nuc-lear."

166. Perscription vs. Prescription

> **Don't Say:** Per-scrip-tion.
> **Say Instead:** Pre-scrip-tion (pruh-scrip-shun).

Think of "pre" in its sense as "before." You need the prescription before you can get better. The same thing applies to the verb—it's never "per-scribe," it's always "pre-scribe."

167. Prespiration vs. Perspiration

> **Don't Say:** Pre-spi-ra-tion.
> **Say Instead:** PER-spi-ra-tion.

Don't substitute "pre" for "per" when you're talking about perspiring. "Per-spi-ra-tion."

168. Disasterous vs. Disastrous

> **Don't Say:** Di-sas-ter-ous.
> **Say Instead:** Di-sas-trous (di-zass-truss, three syllables, not four).

Don't throw a "ter" in there, even though the word clearly comes from "disaster." It's "di-sas-trous."

169. Accidently vs. Accidentally

> **Don't Say:** Ac-ci-dent-ly.
> **Say Instead:** Ac-ci-den-tal-ly (five syllables).

In a flip-flop from the previous explanation, here we need to keep the "tal" from "accidental" when we make the word "ac-ci-den-tal-ly."

170. Representive vs. Representative

> **Don't Say:** Rep-re-sen-tive.
> **Say Instead:** Rep-re-sen-ta-tive (five syllables).

Don't leave out the "ta." It's "rep-re-sen-ta-tive."

171. Preform vs. Perform

> **Don't Say:** Pre-form.
> **Say Instead:** Per-form.

It's "per," not "pre," to start off words about showing off your talents: per-form, per-for-mance, per-for-ming.

172. Asterik vs. Asterisk

> **Don't Say:** As-te-rik or as-te-riks.
> **Say Instead:** As-ter-isk (as-tuh-rik).

Boy, does this one give people trouble! The little star you use to tell a reader that there's a note elsewhere on the page is an as-te-<u>risk</u> (*), with the word "risk" tacked on to the end. Not "as-ter-ix." Not "as-ter-ick." It's "as-te-<u>risk</u>."

173. Artic vs. Arctic

Don't Say: <u>Ar</u>-tic
Say Instead: <u>Arc</u>-tic.

You need the "c" in there—"ar<u>c</u>-tic."

174. Anartica vs. Antarctica

Don't Say: <u>An</u>-<u>ar</u>-ti-ca
Say Instead: <u>Ant</u>-<u>arc</u>-ti-ca.

The first syllable is "ant' with a "t." The second syllable is "arc" with a "c." "<u>Ant</u>-<u>arc</u>-ti-ca."

175. Expresso vs. Espresso

Don't Say: <u>Ex</u>-pres-so.
Say Instead: <u>Es</u>-pres-so (ess-PRESS-oh).

When you're ordering coffee that will keep you up all night, the first syllable of the word isn't "ex," it's "es." "<u>Es</u>-pres-so."

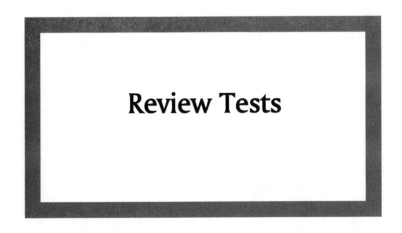

Review Tests

So, you've gone through one of the chapters, and now you want a real challenge. We've included review tests for some of the tougher grammar units in the program:

- ❑ Perplexing Pronouns
- ❑ Vexing Verbs
- ❑ Ambiguous Agreements
- ❑ Mangled Modifiers
- ❑ Problem Prepositions
- ❑ Confused Connections

These tests can help you determine whether the lessons you've learned are really sticking. (See the Introduction for advice on when exactly you should take the tests.) Each review test is followed immediately by an answer key that gives the answers and brief explanations. Good luck!

Chapter 1: Perplexing Pronouns Test

Please circle the correct choice.

1. The bank teller declared that the man at the head of the line and (I, me) would have to leave if we didn't stop singing.

2. I was seated directly between Frank and (she, her) at dinner when they were throwing rolls at each other.

3. We saw Zelda and (he, him) sneaking into the health food store for a quick tofu fix.

4. We thought that (them, their) sneaking around was pointless since everyone knew about their tofu habit.

5. We realized Zelda and (he, him) had no idea they were being watched.

6. Ivan will hire a decorator (who, whom) will promise to refrain from using mauve.

7. Ivan will hire a decorator (who, whom) he can trust with his pit bull, Killer.

8. Ivan will hire (whoever, whomever) gives him the best estimate, but only if Killer approves.

9. Umberto, (who, whom) we'd thought was still in Tibet, appeared yesterday on our doorstep.

10. The car (that, which) you just passed says "Police" on it.

11. Shelley's car, (that, which) is a peculiar eggplant color, cost enough to finance the national debt.

12. Stefano will be working closely with my colleagues and (I, me, myself) to create our new line of designer tweezers.

13. It was (she, her) (who, whom) you saw last night carousing in the moonlight with Dexter and (I, me).

14. May we ask Mildred and (you, yourself) to mind the baby while we're out?

15. Though the baby usually adores (whoever, whomever) she sees, she screamed at our last sitter, (who, whom) we think played the tuba all night.

16. The wig (that, which) we found in the car is much longer and curlier than the wig (that, which) Miriam lost last week.

17. We were petrified by (him, his) sledding so close to the edge of the cliff.

18. The astronomer (who, whom) discovered the comet will name it after either her husband or (whoever, whomever) was bringing her coffee that night.

Answer Key for Chapter 1 Test

1. I. Subject of "would have to leave."
2. her. Object of the preposition "between."
3. him. Object of the verb "saw."
4. their. We didn't think that they were pointless in general, just that the sneaking around was pointless. Thus "sneaking around" is the subject of "was," and "their" modifies "sneaking."
5. he. Subject of "had no idea."
6. who. Subject of "will promise"; if we were using a personal pronoun, we'd say "<u>he</u> will promise."
7. whom. Object of "trust": "Ivan can trust <u>him</u>."
8. whoever. Subject of "gives." The entire second clause, "whoever gives him the best estimate" is the object of "hire"; within that clause, "whoever" is the subject of gives: "<u>he</u> gives Ivan the best estimate."
9. who. Subject of "was": "We'd thought <u>he</u> was still in Tibet."
10. that. Restrictive clause providing information essential to understanding *which car*; referring to a thing.
11. which. Nonrestrictive clause referring to a thing ("car").
12. me. Object of the preposition "with."
13. she (subjective after "to be "), whom (object of the verb "saw": "you saw <u>her</u> carousing"); me (object of the preposition "with").
14. you. Subject of the infinitive "to mind."
15. whomever (object of the verb "sees": "she sees <u>them</u>"); who (subject of the verb "played": we think <u>she</u> played the tuba).

237

16. that, that. Both restrictive clauses referring to a thing (wig).

17. his. We were petrified not by him in general, but by the action of sledding close to the edge of a cliff. "Sledding" is thus the object of "by," and "his" modifies sledding.

18. who (subject of the verb "discovered": "she discovered the comet"), whoever (subject of the verb "was"; the entire last clause, "either her husband or whoever was bringing her coffee" is the object of the preposition "after," but within that clause, "whoever" is the subject of "was ": "he was bringing her coffee").

Chapter 2: Vexing Verbs Test

Please circle the correct choice.

1. After Patrick had (drank, drunk) the third milk shake, he (lay, laid) on the couch for an hour without speaking.

2. Heidi had just (dived, dove) off the side of the pool when she remembered it had been drained for cleaning.

3. Tom absently (set, sat) the TV remote on the couch, forgot about it, and then (set, sat) on it five minutes later.

4. What Jody hadn't (did, done) was to (be sure and, be sure to) lock the gate before the wolves (sprang, sprung) through it.

5. Jean-Paul has cleverly concealed his crime by (lying, laying) a mat over that unfortunate stain on the floor.

6. Jasmine had been studying till her head (swam, swum) and her ears (rang, rung).

7. The enraged mob had already (hang, hung, hanged) Dangerous Dave, but we found his henchmen (lying, laying) in their cells.

8. Jane wished she (was, were) wearing a less extraordinary hat.

9. Elizabeth had never (drived, drove, driven) so fast before, and she liked it so much that she (sang, sung) at the top of her lungs.

10. If Mary (was, were) here yesterday, she won't be coming in today.

11. Kitty's eyes (swam, swum) with tears as she (lay, laid) down the romance novel.

12. Lydia demanded that George (eat, eats) more quickly so they could wash up in time for her favorite show.

13. That banana peel has (laid, lain) on the floor for hours, but no one's slipped on it yet.

14. Jim (hang, hung, hanged) his hat on door, (sat, set) down his boots, and (drank, drunk) a tall, cool root beer float.

15. If I (was, were) safe at home right now, I wouldn't be having half as much fun.

16. We've (swam, swum) so much today that I'm surprised we haven't turned into fish.

17. I suggest that he (lie, lies, lay, lays) his clothes out neatly before packing for the trip.

Answer Key for Chapter 2 Test

1. drunk (past perfect of "drink"), lay (past of "lie").

2. dived. Past of "dive."

3. set (past of "set"), sat (past of "sit").

4. done (past perfect of "did"), be sure to (infinitive with "be sure"), sprang (past of spring).

5. laying. Present participle of "lay."

6. swam (past of "swim"), rang (past of "ring").

7. hanged (past perfect of "hang," special form for executions), lying (present participle of "lie").

8. were. Subjunctive; wish.

9. driven (past perfect of "drive"), sang (past of "sing").

10. was. Indicative; the speaker is not describing a condition contrary to fact (which would require the subjunctive "were") but is explaining what effect will follow from something has already happened.

239

11. swam (past of "swim"), laid (past of "lay").
12. eat. Subjunctive; demand.
13. lain. Present perfect of "lie."
14. hung (past of "hang"), set (past of "set"), drank (past of "drink").
15. were. Subjunctive; condition contrary to fact.
16. swum. Present perfect of "swim."
17. lay. Subjunctive form of "lay" in a sentence offering a suggestion.

Chapter 3: Ambiguous Agreements Test

Please circle the correct choice.

1. Edmund and Daphne (has, have) never taken a vacation without their 10 children.
2. The chair with the scarlet cushions and the five spiral-shaped legs (is, are) a family heirloom.
3. Either that chair or the sofas that clash with it (has, have) got to go.
4. Either the carpenters or the plumber who brought his three assistants (has, have) turned the kitchen upside down.
5. Either Bob or the women in the green car (has, have) knocked over our mailbox this morning.
6. Either the fish or the chicken (was, were) bought fresh this morning, but neither of them (look, looks) very appetizing.
7. Neither your cousins nor Uncle George (has, have) come to the wedding, but all of them (has, have) sent the happy couple a toaster.
8. Each boy and girl in the class (has, have) been given a part in the play, although some of them (is, are) only playing trees and therefore (has, have) no lines.
9. Every rug in this house (needs, need) to be cleaned professionally.

10. Their rock-climbing expedition will be a short one, because all of them (has, have) forgotten to bring rope.

11. None of the pasta (is, are) ready to be served because everyone in the kitchen (keep, keeps) eating it.

12. Somebody left (their, his or her) lurid novel on this seat.

13. Each of the hotels (have, has) an excellent view of either the beach or the factory.

14. Hello, emergency? Someone who can capture hungry bears (need, needs) to come to 31 Maple Street right away.

15. Both the weight machine and the exercise bicycle (was, were) fine pieces of equipment, but I threw them out because neither of them (was, were) being used.

16. Everyone (knows, know) that neither Tom nor Heidi (has, have) the least idea what (they are, he or she is) doing.

17. Anyone who (volunteer, volunteers) to clean this room will get to keep anything (they, he or she) (find, finds).

18. All of the violinists (play, plays) with the orchestra for two hours and (practice, practices) on (their, his or her) own time.

19. Everyone who (bring, brings) (their, his or her) gun (have to, has to) check it at the door.

Answer Key for Chapter 3 Test

1. have. Compound subject with "and."

2. is. The subject, "chair," is singular; everything between "chair" and the verb modifies "chair" and thus can't influence the verb. No matter how many cushions and legs the chair has, it's still one chair: *the chair is a family heirloom.*

3. have. Either/or, closest subject ("sofas") is plural; "that clash with it" modifies "sofa."

4. has. Either/or, closest subject ("plumber") is singular; "who brought his three assistants" modifies "plumber."

5. have. Either/or, closest subject ("women") is plural; "in the green car" modifies "women."

6. was. (Either/or, closest subject ["chicken"] is singular); looks ("neither" is the singular subject).

7. has (neither/nor; closest subject ["Uncle George"] is singular); have ("all" takes a singular or plural verb depending on the meaning of the sentence; here we're referring to a countable number of people, so the verb is plural).

8. has ("each" takes a singular verb), are, have ("some" takes a singular or plural verb depending on the meaning of the sentence, and here we're referring to a countable number of boys and girls, so the verbs are plural).

9. needs. "Every" takes a singular verb.

10. have. "All" takes a singular or plural verb depending on the meaning of the sentence; here, we're referring to a countable number of people, so the verb is plural.

11. is, keeps. "None" takes a singular or plural verb depending on the meaning of the sentence; here, we're referring to the pasta as a whole, so the verb is singular. "Everyone" is singular, so we use the singular verb "keeps."

12. his or her. "Somebody" is singular, so other pronouns referring to it must be singular too. You can avoid "his or her" by rewriting: "Somebody left a lurid novel on this seat."

13. has. "Each" takes a singular verb.

14. needs. "Someone" is the singular subject; "who can capture hungry bears" modifies "someone."

15. were (compound subject with "and"), was ("neither" takes a singular verb).

16. knows ("everyone" takes a singular verb), has ("neither" takes a singular verb), he or she (because "neither" is singular, then pronouns referring back to it must be singular too; you may avoid "he or she" by rewriting: *Everyone knows that <u>Tom and Heidi haven't</u> the least idea what <u>they're</u> doing.*

17. volunteers ("anyone" takes a singular verb), he or she, finds (because "anyone" is singular, then pronouns and verbs referring back to it must be singular too; you may avoid "he or she" by rewriting: *Volunteers to clean this room will get to keep everything they find.*

18. play, practice ("all" takes a singular or plural verb depending on the sentence's meaning; here, we're talking about a quantifiable number of distinct violinists, so the verbs are plural), their (because "all" is plural in this case, pronouns referring back to it must be plural too).

19. brings, his or her, has to. "Everyone" is singular, so everything that follows must be singular too. To avoid "his or her," you may rewrite: *All bandits who bring their guns have to check them at the door.*

Chapter 4: Mangled Modifiers Test

Please circle the correct choice.

1. He felt so (bad, badly) after their fight that he did the dishes for a week, and he apologized so (good, well) that she considered forgiving him.

2. (Near, nearly) 20 clowns came out of that Volkswagen.

3. This is the (bigger, biggest) collection of Jesse James memorabilia in the whole world.

4. Which of the twins is (less, least) likely to be happy living above the garage?

5. Francesca is in the happy position of choosing (between, among) five different suitors; she's decided to accept the one who is the (better, best) dancer.

6. If Francesca were choosing only (between, among) Dexter and Gordon, however, she'd pick the one with (more, the most) money.

7. The (fewer, less) happy Bob is, the more work he does.

8. We found (fewer, less) fish in the pond than we'd hoped, but the (number, amount) of old tires in the water was staggering.

9. The relationships (between, among) the three of us have a convoluted history going back for 20 years.

10. There is a direct relationship (between, among) how loudly you snore and how irritable I get.

11. Of all the children in the class, Hector is the (smartest, most smartest) but also the (less pleasant, least pleasant, least pleasantest).

12. Of all the vases in my apartment, the one shaped like a pig in a tuxedo is (unique, the most unique).

13. Those heavy-duty fish tongs are (the most perfect, the perfect) gift for Steve.

14. Pitching a perfect ball game is the (ultimate, penultimate) achievement for a baseball player.

15. I won't let you leave elementary school to join the circus, and I refuse to discuss this subject any (further, farther).

16. (Hopefully, I hope that) Egore will never drop by unannounced again.

17. She's (plenty, very) lucky to get so much good advice from her mother.

18. (Regretfully, I'm sorry that) we have no patent leather pumps in your size; we do, however, have a fine selection of work boots today.

Answer Key for Chapter 4 Test

1. bad, well.
2. Nearly.
3. biggest.
4. less.
5. among, best.

6. between, more.

7. less.

8. fewer, number.

9. among.

10. between.

11. smartest, least pleasant.

12. unique.

13. the perfect.

14. ultimate.

15. further. Conservative speakers prefer "further" for a quantity that can't be measured.

16. I hope that. "Hopefully" is widely used, widely understood, and useful, but conservative speakers object to it.

17. very.

18. I'm sorry that. "Regretfully" is, like "hopefully," widely used and useful; but very conservative speakers object to it.

Chapter 5: Problem Prepositions Test

Please circle the correct choice.

1. Horace (agrees to, agrees with) store the limburger in his refrigerator, but he doesn't (agree to, agree with) your theory that limburger is best preserved unwrapped.

2. I strongly (differ with, differ from) Egbert on the question of how Martians (differ with, differ from) human beings.

3. I still don't see how your new job is (different from, different than) the last one.

4. Our ongoing feud (centers on, centers around) his refusal to make more coffee when he's drunk the last cup.

5. Reginald certainly hoped his new dungeon would be (different from, different than) the one where he'd languished for so long.

6. When I asked them where the nearest gas station (was, was at), they said I should have found one before entering Death Valley.

7. Get (off, off of) that stage this minute and go back to the office where you belong!

8. Have you been warned (as to, about) his tendency to do the cha-cha in his sleep?

Answer Key for Chapter 5 Test

1. agrees to, agree with.
2. differ with, differ from.
3. different from.
4. centers on.
5. different from.
6. was.
7. off.
8. about.

Chapter 6: Confused Connections Test

Please circle the correct choice or rewrite according to instructions.

Use "not only/but also" to link the following sentence:

1. I'm so delighted that I'll praise you to the skies. I'll bake you a cake.

Use "on the one hand/on the other hand" to link sentences in questions 2, 3, and 4:

2. Irving has an amazing computer. He has no notion how it works.

3. Deborah's feet are on the ground. Deborah's head is in the clouds.

4. My stomach is growling. My heart is singing. My mind is wandering.

246

5. You can give me either a tie for my birthday (or, or maybe) a gold-plated yacht.

6. Neither the policeman, who had a slight limp, (or, nor) the startled onlookers could stop the thief who snatched Vivian's ruby hat pin.

7. As exhausted (as, that) they were, they played Ping-Pong obsessively into the small hours of the night.

   Include "because" when rewriting the following sentence:

8. The reason you can't see Alphonso is because he's hiding from you behind the curtains.

   Rewrite the sentences in 9 and 10, replacing "per" with a more precise connector:

9. Per this report card, you're failing in spelling and arithmetic.

10. Per your inquiry, we have sought a reason for this regulation and found none.

11. I never want to see you again, (and, plus) I never even want to see your house again.

12. We wondered (as to whether, whether) we had ever laughed so hard at a budget meeting before.

    Rewrite this sentence, replacing "in the event that" with a more precise connector:

13. In the event that the liquid in this test tube turns orange and starts to smoke, drop everything and run before it explodes.

    Rewrite this sentence, replacing "owing to the fact that" with a more precise connector:

14. At the end of his act, Chip couldn't pull a rabbit out of a hat owing to the fact that the rabbit had eaten the hat.

15. "Gapers' delay" (is where, means that) there's a traffic jam (due to the fact that, because) drivers slow down to gape at something off the road.

Answer Key for Chapter 6 Test

1. I'm so delighted that I will not only praise you to the skies, but also bake you a cake.

2. On the one hand, Irving has an amazing computer, but on the other hand, he has no notion how it works.

3. On the one hand, Deborah's feet are on the ground, but on the other hand, her head is in the clouds.

4. On the one hand, my stomach is growling and my mind is wandering, but on the other hand, my heart is singing. *Or:* On the one hand, my heart is singing, but on the other hand, my stomach is growling and my mind is wandering. *(Remember, you can't have three hands!)*

5. or.

6. nor.

7. as.

8. You can't see Alphonso because he's hiding from you behind the curtains.

9. According to this report card, you're failing in spelling and arithmetic.

10. In response to your inquiry, we have sought a reason for this regulation and found none.

11. and.

12. whether.

13. If the liquid in this test tube turns orange and starts to smoke, drop everything and run before it explodes.

14. At the end of his act, Chip couldn't pull a rabbit out of a hat because the rabbit had eaten the hat.

15. means that, because.

Index

249

About the Author and Editor

Ann Batko is a business communications expert and a former Executive Editor of Rand McNally & Company. During her 20-year career, she has trained advertising, marketing, and publishing executives in effective writing and presentation skills. She lives in the Chicago area with her daughter, whom she is currently instructing on the proper uses of the subjunctive mood.

Edward Rosenheim is the David B. and Clara E. Stern Professor Emeritus in the Department of English Language and Literature at the University of Chicago, where he taught for 42 years. Dr. Rosenheim is a Jonathan Swift scholar and has written a number of important books, articles, and reviews on this subject. For 20 years he was the editor of the prestigious journal *Modern Philology*.